Ish River Country

Poems from
Ish River Country

Collected Poems and Translations

Robert Sund

Shoemaker Hoard

This first paperback edition is published by
Shoemaker & Hoard in collaboration
with The Poet's House Trust.

Copyright © 2004 by Poet's House Trust

Cover painting by Robert Sund, from the
collection of Joan Cross. Author photograph
by Mary Rardlett, MSCUA, University of
Washington Libraries, used with permission.

Library of Congress Cataloging-in-Publication Data
Sund, Robert, 1929–2001
Poems from Ish River country : collected poems & translations / Robert Sund.
p. cm.
I. Title.
PS3569.U5P64 2004
811'.54--dc22   2004011914

ISBN 978-0-912887-28-9

Pleasure Boat Studio: A Literary Press
201 West 89 Street
New York, NY 10024

www.pleasureboatstudio.com/pleasboat@nyc.rr.com
Originally published by Shoemaker & Hoard

10   9   8   7   6   5   4   3   2   1

Contents

2. Ish River (1983)

Acknowledgments

The trustees of the Robert Sund Poet's House wish to acknowledge and thank the editors and publishers who first brought many of the poems collected here into print: the late Don Ellegood of University of Washington Press, Jack Shoemaker (formerly) of North Point Press, Rusty North of Sagittarius Press, Jerry Reddan of Tangram Press, Sam Hamill of Copper Canyon Press and Steve Herold of Double Elephant Press.

Thanks to Chip Hughes and Tim McNulty for their work compiling and editing this manuscript. And a special thanks to Jack Shoemaker, Trish Hoard and the staff at Shoemaker & Hoard for their enthusiasm, care and commitment to bringing this book into print.

Grateful acknowledgment is made to the family of Rabbe Enckell for permission to publish translations from the poet's work.

Publication is made possible with assistance from the Robert Sund Poet's House Trust.

The Robert Sund Poet's House is a not-for-profit organization established to promote the work and vision of poet, painter and musician Robert Sund. To learn how you can become part of this effort, or to find out more about the Robert Sund Poet's House, visit our web site at www.robertsundpoetshouse.org.

Preface

"Ish River" —
    like breath,
    like mist rising from a hillside.
Duwamish, Snohomish, Stillaguamish, Samish,
Skokomish, Skykomish . . . all the ish rivers.

I live in the Ish River country
between two mountain ranges where
many rivers
run down to an inland sea.

R. S.

March 29, 1979
Cloud House

1

Bunch Grass

In memory of my teacher,
Theodore Roethke (1908-63)

What happens here in mankind
is matched by what happens out there
in the history of grass and wheat. . . .

Emerson

Part One

1

In wheat country
for miles
telephone wires and power lines
loop
between thin poles
standing across the country like people
saying the same things to one another over and over.
Sitting on a wire,
one bird
keeps it from happening.

2

Dark leaves lift in light wind.
At dawn, dew
slips away from hidden cloisters in the grass.
Near a bed of lupine
the meadowlark sees his shadow
wakening beside him.
There,
among the lavender blue spires
balanced
surely upon the light blossom of wonder,
he tries to remember
but can recall
only part of a song he must have once
known fully,
and he sings again.

3

Women who marry into wheat
look out kitchen windows
seeing
nothing but wheat.
Under locust trees in the back yard
beautiful city streets spring alive,
night streets
radiant with glowing lights that brighten
as each new shining locust blossom
falls
into the dust and tall dry grass
where
for months
no rain fell.

4

In a landscape that desperately needs color
why do the flowers
stay
so close to the ground?
You meet them with surprise
hidden
in the pale grasses.

5

I sit on a rickety bench just outside
the elevator door,
hoping to see things clearly.
Already the sun is up far enough to be hot,
and shadows
slower than an eye has patience for
begin to leave the hilly fields.
In the air
only a little of the morning remains.
At the base of the elevator,
in one corner,
a piece of chaff twirls around in the wind;
tumbles, pulls, and twirls,
in a spider's
abandoned
web.

6

Looking out through the wide elevator doors
into miles of hot, wavering
southeast Washington wheat fields,
saturated and near boredom,
each of us expects the other to break silence.
I begin.
"John. Describe these wheat fields.
Gentle, hilly, not flat.
How would you do it?"
Oceans of sunlight wash over in the long space
before he speaks.
"It's hard. Everyone thinks of Kansas."

7

Today, instead of sleeping through the noon hour when there are no trucks, I had a talk with the foreman of the railroad section gang. They're out here unloading a boxcar full of grain doors. The foreman and his helper and I leaned on the bed of his old International pickup while four other men unloaded the grain doors and stacked them along the tracks. We talked a good deal, about people, how they live the way they do, and why. I listened to the two of them for a while without saying anything. They were using more than the customary amount of railroad jargon, for my benefit—a little proud of it, and contented within themselves.

"What's a spot bar?" I asked.

Jake, the foreman, is a short heavy man under his striped bib overalls and baseball cap. The other man spat down into the dust and looked over at Jake to hear what he'd say.

"Well, say you've got to take a dip out of the track. Well, you use a spot bar. It's got black and white stripes on it, and one man stands off with it so the other fella can sight up. Two points makes a straight line, light travels, and you know . . . all that."

The other man interrupts to say that he never could work with somebody he calls "old Jim." Jim couldn't use a sight bar if the Union Pacific president made a special trip out to watch him do it.

"Well," says Jake, "Jim's a grandma, is all."

There is a silence between us. The fact registers there without extravagant emotion.

We talk for a while longer, and when I look away into the distant fields, Jake says: "It's sure been a long time since I seen a philosophical young fella like you."

He agrees with a point I made about people not need-ing to have so much, and wasting themselves because they don't learn that. I remember having said: "Rule out everything arbitrary—money, happiness, the future. All these things." Having made his compliment to me, he is pleased to have said it out loud. I'm slightly embarrassed and say, in an inverted manner I have less of now than I used to: "Well, you've got your eyes open too." People should compliment one another. The old epics are full of lengthy, elaborated compliments. Think of an epic, and one man is saying something about another.

Before he goes, I learn the name of the plant fre-quented by butterflies.

"That's Star Thistle," he says. "But I suppose there's a more high-priced name for it if you knew what it was. Funny thing about that, it don't grow where the land's cultivated; mostly just on the main line. They call that Star Thistle, near as I know."

8

Star Thistle, Jim Hill Mustard, White Tops,
Chinese Lettuce, Pepper Grass.
The names of things
bring them
closer.

9

A dusty black beetle
walks over the concrete floor.
He tries to hurry, but hasn't the energy
to drag his body along.
His head is too small, and he has been going
back and forth through the same country for minutes,
wanting a place to burrow down.
The scant
piles of wheat are not deep enough, but he
burrows anyway,
back legs flicking the air.
At last he backs out, he has learned enough,
and wanders
over the concrete floor again,
a poor, unclassifiable creature who, as he walks,
draws neither tears nor laughter.
An old man driving truck for Dickinson
says, when I ask him
the beetle's name,
"All I ever heard 'em called
since I was a kid
was a stink bug."
He reflects on that, and says:
"That don't give 'em
much of a chance, does it!"

Looking absurd as a near-sighted scholar,
a grasshopper
clings to a short blade of grass.
Having climbed so far out into space,
and finding the grass
too insubstantial to jump from,
but enough to hold him,
he climbs
slowly backwards,
then
steps off onto the ground,
and disappears.

Harvest at its peak,
the heaviest day we've had,
truckloads of wheat and barley keep coming
into the elevator and out again
all day long.
Acting like truckdrivers,
men swing down out of truck cabs,
stand waiting until their trucks are emptied,
then swing back up
and are gone.
Sixteen miles away
where the wheat fields dwindle,
in shady cabins at the edge of town,
wives are cooking greasy food
and saying
shut up, shut up, shut up,
to children who may one day
understand how we stand upside down
on scales never meant for
the human creature
we must become.

12

At the top of the elevator,
in the half light of a dusty shaft
we're working quietly,
breathing barley dust and repairing a worn motor;
patient, careful;
surprised the way we handle it.
Somewhere
in a big city
a poet is
writing phrases
about beautiful children of the poor,
ugly machines.

13

A bee thumps against the dusty window,
falls to the sill,
climbs back up, buzzing;
falls again;
and does this over and over.
If only he would climb higher!
The top half of the window is
open.

14

First there is silence; then,
farther on,
at the edge of a field,
the riddled song of a cricket. Beyond that,
silence.
And still beyond, barely audible,
the hum of a combine
going uphill through rows of wheat.
No wind at all.
The sky is a sailboat,
scarcely moving.

15

The rolling hills of wheat expect nothing.
They don't move,
left to themselves.
On a crest, several miles away,
a combine comes into view
and stops.
Yellow combine, yellow wheat.
A tiny red and green truck pulls up alongside it.
There are still some people around.

16

At five-thirty in the afternoon, the wind
is making ready to leave the wheat fields again.
Outside the elevator
the steady man sits on a bench
pretending his life is full.
He is listening for
something inside himself.
A truck comes down the road.
It's several miles away and we can't see it yet,
but he lifts his head slowly and says:
"That's the Dodge. A load of barley comin'."
Early today
we talked about books.
He has a sister who likes to read.
Poetry eludes him,
the sense of it.
I tell him he has an ear for trucks, it's only
a matter of preference.
"Well," he says, "I don't know about that."
The truck comes in.
I weigh it, Gross, Tare, Net.
The driver stands just outside in the shade
drinking water from a jug.
He walks back in, initials the receipt, "L.A.,"
and leaves without a word.
He has hardly spoken a word all summer.
Barley dust fills the air,
eyes burn from it, skin itches in sleeves
and sweaty shirt collars.
The truck fades away down the road.
We're standing in the cleared air again.

17

After each truck fine dust settles on the floor.
Where we walked, there are our footprints.
John sweeps them away.
Faint streaks of dust linger behind the broom,
like a stream.
A far-off cricket cries.
Tufts of grass
are falling asleep.
In a quick gust the scoop shovel
swings out from the concrete wall,
falls back,
and a dusty ghost of itself
vanishes before it reaches the floor.

Part Two

18

America is a strange man
lying in a wheat field.
Combines
are coming in the distance,
gearing down
to take the hill.
Nothing
will stop them.
Working fourteen hours a day,
three weeks now
without a day's rest, the combine men
are tired, and praying
for rain.
Lying in the wheat,
the strange man
turns over on his side.
In his hand
a clod of dirt
crumbles.

19

There's a beetle walking on the ground below me,
looking for passage beyond my shoe.
Sir,
take a promise:
I'll know you yet.
We're going somewhere together,
soon.

Beneath an intensely hot sun
new
landscapes hover and shimmer in the air.
And so,
all the flowers
(pink, dusty blue, yellow, nameless colors)
run back and forth
in and out the fenceposts skirting a field,
rioting with
laughter among themselves because
a wandering, stone-deaf butterfly
dropped in mid-flight
to rest between two rows of stubble,
choosing
a clod of dirt.

21

Between incoming trucks
we're loading a boxcar to ship out.
Atop the elevator, wheat
bangs out of a scale, six hundred pounds
every thirty seconds.
It pours down through eighty feet of pipe
and splashes inside
against the boxcar's wooden walls.
Fine dust flies out,
alive with silvery particles that drift
glinting through a shaft of sunlight.
When there are no trucks to weigh,
I write brief poems
to strike a balance and keep
the day
from toppling over.

22

With a sandwich
halfway out of a wax bag, I sit
in the shade
enjoying a quiet lunch.
A fly comes around, close.
Too close.
I'm trying to act nonchalant—
a form of charity.
By some freak he gets inside the bag.
Carefully,
I pull out my liver-and-onion sandwich.
I've got him!
I lay the bag down, bring my fist
down hard, but
the bag splits open,
he's gone.
Another
failure.

23

Just outside the elevator
in the hot sun,
you hear
the slow lament of flies.
Listening closely,
you hear also,
just under them—
it might be miles away—
the wind,
soft,
and steady.
It's lunchtime in the fields.
Combines are cooling off.

24

It's surprising how many
people are laughing, once you get away
from universities
and stop reading newspapers.
This morning,
Sam described his boss.
"After harvest, he
goes down there on the beach, down at
Seaside, Oregon, and he watches them
      girls . . ."
The barley
pours out of his truck, into the pit,
making noise and raising dust.
When it's quiet,
he repeats, with a wry look, "Yeah,
just watches them girls,
they got them short shorts on."
He cocks his head sideways,
making the gesture he sees in his mind:
"Like a bulldog lookin' at a phonograph."

25

Late afternoon, there's a restlessness in the air.
Five or six small whirlwinds of dust
rise up in the road,
move quickly up and down it,
then cross over into sweet clover,
settling down.

26

From the southwest
comes a high moaning wind,
"a regular Wallowa," the old ranchers call it.
Dry plants are flung into the air,
the country turns wild.
Sweet clover
whips against the ground,
clouds of dust
peel off the summer fallow, and
as the dust thickens
the world grows smaller,
a fearful thing.
Grass
panics, running in one direction,
a multitude.
Tribes of ancient Indians come riding
over the hills,
they rage in the powdery summer fallow,
they never stop coming, and dust
rises in their wake, obliterating hill after hill
into dust-clouded distances,
chanting,
paced and low,
Wallowa . . . Wallowa . . . Wallowa . . .

*". . . Theodore Roethke, Pulitzer Prize winner
and one of America's great poets,
died today. . . ."*

Five o'clock news on the radio

Cursing,
picking stones up,
how long I don't know,
and flinging them through the air,
I've finally stopped.
The last stone I threw down the gravel road
bounced against a few other stones,
little puffs of dust rose up,
and down the road a ways, the stone,
though it might have bounced a little farther,
stopped, still.
I couldn't find that same stone again
if I tried.
Where it lies, it lies
with stone's capacity,
and with that much
eloquence.

28

A dirt-crusted green jeep turns off the highway,
crosses the railroad tracks,
and drives part way up to the elevator.
The man walks
slowly up to us, half with caution,
half boldly,
feigning composure.
Inside the jeep a dog is barking.
Do we know
anybody around that needs a ranch hand?
He guards his disappointment,
thanks us,
and drives away.
Crickets plague the stubbled fields,
their songs travel
in low, thin lines through the wheat.

Seven o'clock. One day is gone,
August 1, 1963.
The meadowlark gives into this sultry evening air
songs
beautifully cool and clear as water.
Carefully he spaces each one.
Somewhere Roethke will soon lie in the ground.
Lark songs,
and burial; these incomprehensible poles
cradle us
a whole life
long.

30

Through a wide field of stubble
trots a black dog, nose down, scooping the air as he goes
farther into the field, black and alone.

31

Now as the sun sets, cricket songs
begin to rise straight up,
thin black stalks rising into the air,
holding up
invisible buds of song which open
out, into the silence.

PART THREE

32

There is no wind. What was the wind like
yesterday when it blew?
Nothing moves, for mile after mile, nothing moves.
I watch a stalk of grass nearby. Nothing.
I expect a leaf of sweet clover to stir.
Stillness everywhere.
And then
in a kind of glory,
out of a spray of alfalfa a bee flies away
into the distance,
lost.
The leaf he sat on shifts back into place.

33

Two white
butterflies are doing a jig,
going higher and
higher.
Is it
a rancher and his money?
Myself and what I'm looking for?
Or two white butterflies
alone?

34

Five magpies
stand in a circle at the edge of the road,
like old jobless men leaning on a pier,
looking down into the glazed water,
each one about to
reveal the secrets of his past.
A wheat truck roars by.
The magpies
leap clumsily into the air and disperse,
leaving behind
the body of a pheasant.
In the truck's wake, one wing rises like a sail,
then falls slack.
A few loose feathers
catch light gusts of wind
and glide
over the scattered wheat and gravel.

35

A wheat rancher drives up in his air-conditioned GMC
station wagon, nothing special on his mind. Tired of
harvests, he wants to talk. He talks about a skinflint
friend of his who's trying to raise some beef cattle on
poor ground.

"Why, up there, if she's gonna get any feed at all,
a cow's gotta have a mouth three feet wide and travel
thirty miles an hour."

Each day fewer fields remain, fewer trucks come into the elevator. There are only two ranchers still harvesting. We're busy shipping out boxcars of wheat and barley to make room in the bins for the grain still to come in from the fields. And the sense of things over and done with hovers in the air around us. I write little these last few days. I have already begun not seeing the countryside around me. I will pray now, twice. Once to see it again; and now, for what I give you.

> Let these poems be like bunch grass,
> in ground winds,
> flash floods, and sunlight,
> holding together
> while one cricket sheltered here
> sings his single song.

37

The ranchers are selling their wheat early this year, not holding it over for a better price in the Spring. Next year the government lifts restrictions on planting, and nobody is sure what will happen when wheat grows "fencerow to fencerow." This morning another man has come out from the Grain Growers to help us out. John and I haven't got time to cooper boxcars and handle trucks too.

At lunchtime, he takes his carpenter's apron off and sits on a grain door in the shade of a boxcar, resting before he eats. I go out to join him and notice a Bible resting on the ledge under the rear window of his car. He says he doesn't read it much, and because he is anxious not to appear narrowly Christian, I want to know more about him. He is sixty-five, about to retire; a lonely man, it seems. There is something unspoken in him. His eyes squint to keep out the bright sunlight falling now just where the boxcar's shadow stops. I say, "There's one thing in Mark that has always puzzled me." He turns to face me, and I continue. "Where Jesus says, *To them that have shall be given, and from them that have not shall be taken away*. That always seemed cruel to me, but since the verb hasn't got an object (have what? have not what?) if you supply an object, it's really alive. Love. Money. Intelligence. Curiosity. Anything."

In the bleached countryside of his mind, suddenly a new season washes over; common plants begin to blossom. And now, ideas fly back and forth between us, like bees, their legs thickening with pollen.

In the next hour we talk a lot and I learn that he has been reading Rufus Jones, Meister Eckhart, and

The Cloud of Unknowing. He nearly trembles with a new joy he kept hidden. His wife writes poetry, he tells me, and adds—thrusting years recklessly aside—"I've worked here sixteen years, one harvest to another. I've seen a lot of young men come and go, and never had a decent conversation. It's worse with the college kids. They don't think, most of them."

Trucks start coming in again, lunch is over. He puts his carpenter's apron on again, but before we part he invites me home to dinner this evening, careful not to spoil it by appearing as happy as he really is.

Back inside the elevator, I'd like to lie down somewhere in a cool, dark corner, and weep. What are people doing with their lives? what are they doing?

38

A fieldmouse
crouches low
nibbling kernels of wheat
left where the combines worked last week.
A shadow the size of a hawk
darkens the stubble
an inch away.
Before he can drop half a kernel to the ground
one claw
sure as steel
gathers in his back.

39

Afternoon,
with just enough of a breeze for him to ride it
lazily, a hawk
sails still-winged
up the slope of a stubble-covered hill,
so low
he nearly
touches his shadow.

40

At one of the ranches there's a hand who once had
a beautiful wife, a family, a good business. Now,
each harvest he comes up from California, alone. He
explains The Fall, gesturing with an imaginary glass:
"Too many highchairs, and not enough money in the
morning."

Here he gets board and room—("Beefsteaks
too, boy, I mean thick, old Cecil feeds good, he ain't
cheap!")—plus twenty dollars a day. ("Twenty-five if ya
catch your own chickens.")

I ask him how he likes his job.

"Like it fine," he says quickly, "but don't forget, kid,
'the worker and the employer have nothing in common.'
That's the Wobblies. Hell, I can recite the preamble
and whole works, beginning to end."

Today he drives into the elevator, dumps his wheat,
his last load this year, and loudly, cheerfully, shouts:
"O.K., boys," as he drives out, "I'll see ya under a leaky
bridge."

41

What day is it now?
Like a star on a moonlit river, my life
graced by an element simple as water,
I move with love and care
where old meanings grow full,
and others lose their hold.
Slowly, I release myself.
From corridors of used and vacant buildings,
I release myself.
The jailor,
shuffling his feet and jingling some keys,
walks farther and farther away,
then disappears.
As though we had made an agreement,
I turn and walk away.
I've wanted to do this all my life!

42

Blooming
in the cinders between railroad ties,
"Star Thistle,"
a plant
spare as a cactus
hoards yellow blossoms among
its prickly stems.
On the most visible blossom, a butterfly
has stopped to rest.
As its white wings beat slowly,
folding over and folding over,
the plant holds up
one pulsing blossom which repeats
white and yellow, white
and yellow,
the rhythm of a tremendous harvest
coming and going.
Somewhere
between the butterfly and the blossom
lies a green field, immense,
and never visited.

43

In Walla Walla, cool streams
come running
from Blue Mountain foothills
to flow inaudibly just under the ground,
and century-old maples and elms reach their roots
down, weaving nets to stop water.
People walk along
hot streets under canvas awnings.
Late in the day,
girls see reflections of themselves
in the glass of store windows.
Out at the State Penitentiary
in a garden as large as a field
one of the inmates
walks down the long rows of lettuce,
carrying a hoe.
He kneels down there, and when
his hand
brushes a leaf,
a green leaf, a soft
and delicate leaf,
what he learns
is misery.

44

Near me,
there's a flutter of birds passing through heaven.
I'm singing in a silent place,
remembering my happiest friends.
I'm a stalk of grass
where the wind is blowing.
You have to
bend close to hear
anything at all.

45

Late tonight
a friend and I have driven up Kibbler Road
in the Blue Mountain foothills.
Walla Walla below us
is a series of strings of lights
laced one over the other,
far away, like
a town under water.
We walk in the dark
through a field of newly plowed-under stubble,
remembering a few of the constellations.
Orion's Belt and the Big Dipper
leap quickly out, and slowly recede,
flattening to a sky full of stars.
Coyotes are howling
up in the mountains.
Something happens
in brittle grass near the roadside ditch;
a badger, maybe.
The air is so still that when we drive back,
dust we stirred on our way up
still hangs over the road.
Winding downward, nearing farmhouses again,
lights on in some of the kitchens,
the road is sprinkled with
blossoms newly fallen out of the locust trees.
A fat porcupine waddles along in the headlights,
and turns off,
slipping through a ridge of tall grass.
The car engine grows louder,
back in town.
Under a drive-in's fluorescent lights
moths bump and flicker
over the tops of cars.

46

Next week I go
back to Seattle.
I think of
gumwrappers slipping over the streets
windy as sailboats, scraping in the night;
old men coughing in rooms;
people safe in the bleak and static average,
enduring
sidewalk monotonies, square on square,
getting no place.
None of this is news.
But does it matter
which end of a sinking ship you stand on?

PART FOUR

47

Dry, bleached kernels of wheat and barley
lie on the ground
beside shoots of green wheat
sprouting in the gravel road.
Tonight,
when no one is here,
doves from the elevator roof
will drift
one by one down
to feed on this scattered grain.
Across the highway,
in a field of recently harvested alfalfa,
sprinklers rhythmically irrigate the field
which turns green again
beneath the broad arches of flung water.
This life, at least, is beautiful.

48

Heavy rain now, darker skies.
Driven rain slants hard against the elevator,
trickles under
the southwest door, and a little stream
winds across the floor,
slow as the Columbia.
Off toward the Blue Mountains, thunder
tumbles through the clouds
and rolls away.
Dark skies.
All the birds have disappeared.
It will be raining out in the Snake River canyons and hills
at lonely crossroads
where mailboxes stand in a row like farmers'
wives, not speaking.
A patch of sunlight flows over the road.
Stones glisten
and small flowers on the banks of roadside ditches
are washed clean.
Except for an ant pivoting on a stone,
jerking in various directions,
drawn on,
not a single creature is moving.
Badgers,
to the sound of rain, fall asleep
in burrows
under the darkening wheat.

49

We've come to town. No harvesting in this weather.
There's no dust here, but when I join the Tempanys
sitting on the front porch of their big Victorian house,
drinking a cold beer, suddenly rain pours down, light-
ning and thunder jolt the ground. The porch is shaken.
Rain in the elm trees, like a surf. After one huge flash
the power goes out. We eat our dinner by candle light.
Later, Roger Cockerline stops by and we go for a drive
over into Oregon. The air is lively with the odor of
musty wheat, almost edible, and whole ranges of blue
light forked with white incandescence cancel out the
night. Clouds leap back and forth. Everywhere light-
ning comes up in unpredictable regions of black sky,
cracking again and again the round black shell of
night. I keep wondering: are we inside the shell, or
outside?

50

At quitting time
a combine clatters unseen behind a hill,
then emerges over the crest,
flowering orange against the sky.
The driver shuts off his engine.
Sweat and dust burn
in his swollen, red-rimmed eyes.
When he climbs off the seat and jumps down,
the field sways beneath him.
He is buried by silence,
lost in it.
Coming down the hill
to where he parked his car in the morning,
he is slowly becoming someone else,
entering another country.
Where he walks,
puffs of dust behind him
turn golden
in slanted sunlight.

51

The fields are wider,
harvest over.
Hot, cloudless skies; and the air is a bubble.
Suddenly, a hawk rising
out of the summer fallow up into
the returning wind
shatters the land for miles around.
Bunch grass flows uphill.
Dragonflies bounce through the air.
A butterfly flies
sideways on the wind, trying not to slide off.
Another falters in mid-flight,
folds her wings, drops,
then flares again, buoyed up in her own delight.
A jet plane
bores a thundering tunnel through the sky,
and behind it
the sky rumbles down, filling the tunnel with silence.
The fields are quiet again,
still as stones
cooling in the grass.
I wish a cricket would sing.
And sing and sing,
and know
why men go
to live on cold mountains.

52

With the sun low,
the shadow of the grain elevator
reaches across a field.
Away at the far end where the shadow narrows,
between itself and the shorn wheat,
its true substance begins.
Birds,
silent the whole day long
when we waited and waited for music,
begin to sing.
First the meadowlark,
then doves on the elevator roof,
and now,
somewhere in a low spot by the nearest hill,
a blackbird
is coming to rest in the air around him,
weaving music into it
before he sleeps.
From a fencepost, the lark—
as though he had waited for just this moment—
sings,
letting each liquid song
seep into
the dry ground.

53

Sharp lines
soften in the reflected light
as the sun falls lower and lower.
Shadows
slowly lift the fields.
Coming from somewhere unseen,
a barn swallow shoots up into the bright sky,
dips down into
the shadows, sweeps
back up,
brilliant and sunlit,
designing
in an old, unformulated language
the single word for
joy.

54

Going home,
driving back to the coast,
I have a prairie sunset
flooding the Horse Heaven Hills.
I had hoped it would be this way,
remembering—
the whole rainy winter long.
Far behind me now,
brown plateaus
streaked with outcroppings of red rock
and burdened with fields of meager grass
step down,
taking centuries
into the Snake River.

2

Ish River

In memory of
my father and mother
my grandfather and grandmother
Evart and Elsa, Johan and Ida
Sund

BOOK I

THE HIDES OF WHITE HORSES
SHEDDING RAIN

Night along the Columbia, Day in Blewett Pass, Going Home

1

Far out on the dark river,
a fish jumps.

Dew is gathering on dry willow branches.

My friend lies asleep,
and I head back to our tents in the locust trees,
a mile away.

Inland,
the river has left a still pond.
A few snipe call back and forth in the night.
Their small tracks in the mud
        fill up with moonlit water.

I think of
anonymous Chinese poets, old poems on silk,
the pleasure of being alone,
walking
through a herd of cows asleep in scant alfalfa,
        the last crop of summer.

2

Over my head, the moon is half in the sky,
half in the locust branches.
Some people are still awake, talking softly.
Our small fire falls to a circle of quiet coals.

Falling asleep,
I trace the long drive home tomorrow; south—
    then west,
      across the mountains.
And someone has mentioned Seattle.

Garbage cans
spill over onto the sidewalk at Tai Tung,
    and the fat cook limps
      back through the screen door, smiling.

Down on the docks
they're unloading a boatful of black-eyed halibut.
A fisherman
seeing the moon on the wet deck
remembers Norway.

3

Along the Columbia,
    three more hours and I'm home.
But first
I close the car door
and walk in a field of mountain grass.

I lie down, drink
clear water, dream of old rituals
and what it feels to be pure of heart.

When I get back home to the Ish River country,
I'll open the barn door
and see the hides of white horses
    shedding rain.

Two Poems from Swede Hill

1

BARN

Suddenly there are ancient odors!
My grandfather's barn!
Pitchforks lean in the far corner,
prongs stuck in old planks.
A dim puddle of oil
      covered with hayseeds and dust
lies under the stored mowing machine.
Cobwebs stretch
between rusted tines of the pitchforks.
At the bottom of a dusty gallon jug,
its cork fallen in,
a mouse
lies on his back,
      twisted in his last breath,
      the unfinished
      gestures of life.

2

HOUSE

My grandmother,
for the joy of hearing the floor creak with
the mysterious feeling of damp cellars,
walks
over the kitchen floor.
Down there
a spider sleeps, legs folded together
      making a witch's hand.
Listen: such silence gathers,

you hear
the generous orange squared heart of a fir beam
releasing a trickle of powder,
little grains falling to fleck the pale white long legs of
    old potatoes
reaching for their youth.

Just Before Sleep, I Dream of My Grandfather Returned to His Farm in the Early Spring

1

Where he stands
halfway out in the field, still as a tree,
he doesn't see me watching
from under a fenceline cedar.
His old clothes weigh heavy on him.
His eyes are hatching something new
     for the one big field
       that always worked him hardest.

Is he thinking tractors, not horses, now?
For in this field
he liked to tromp lopsided in a furrow
behind his horses,
"the best team of whites in Grays Harbor county,"
ploughing.

2

Where the drainage ditch once ran
before its cedar casings rotted
     —a trace of red in the mud—
     water
     lies on the grass
     draining off so slow
     the lightest grasses do not budge.

He knows everything there is
waiting to do.

3

When I slip through the fence,
        bend low over a wire—
a staple pulls out of a post
leaving two dark eyes in the wood.
The wire goes limp
        without a noise.

Alder saplings
no bigger than switches
have come into the field a year before me,
fervent with new leaves.

Standing in the shadow he casts
I am close enough to touch or speak to him.
But no word comes right enough.

4

In a corner of the woodshed near the house
patches of powdery mold
are spreading
over his work shoes.

My Father

1

In America, history goes by quickly.

Like a windstorm.

Finland
is a coat flattened against my father,
        like newspaper
        caught in blackberry.

2

I think of his grave
        in the small cemetery outside Elma,
name and dates
carved in the headstone.
I remember the day he was buried by greedy men.
And the day before:
my mother, my brother and his wife, and I,
upstairs in Whiteside's Funeral Parlor,
followed by the undertaker,
we walked across a lavender carpet
while the pastel lights
sent cheap violins weeping through the air,
trying to break us
between the rows of luxurious coffins.

My mother said, and almost laughed,
"shopping for a coffin,"
before she fell apart, crying in my arms,
trembling into her widowhood.

3

I said: "Dad hated this . . . Let's not let them
        beat him at the last."

That day we chose the cheapest coffin
        this country can make.
I watched the undertaker
wilt into his lavender economy and try to smile.
And my father
grew joyful inside me.

Back out on the street,
my brother shoved the car into second gear,
roaring, "This country
            has gone to hell!"

In the back seat, our mother sat quaking
and holding behind a handkerchief her destroyed mouth.
Over the craggy ridges of the handkerchief
her eyes burned shut
and cracked like ashes in the rain.

For My Brother, Don, at Porter Creek,
in Late February

It is winter, the night wandering away.
And below the leaves that have lain so long in puddles
an unseen life calls
like a voice in a cavern; we are
　　walking in,
　　deeper,
the new light appears huge, light that was
visible in wings of dragonflies
on summer afternoons.

Travelers, hotel rooms,
remember them,
leaves filling up the branches, building
　　the voice we can hear
　　when we stand still next to our shadows.
"It will be
a beautiful spring."
I felt it tonight,
it was being prepared
inside the rose,
the silent shifting of ash in the petals,
in the trees,
in the earth between the waking roots,
the suck of rising water,
and I say
to my brother when he comes so easily to mind again
and I see him standing
on the river bank, steelheading,
the river below him like the swirling air in a chalice,
alone in the wind,
rain hissing where it falls at the edge of his fire:

Wait.
The blood that flows between us.
The smile of your wife, your children,
the hills behind your house,
our father.
Wait.
I will be there with the sound of water,
with the sound of ashes,
with the whipped leaves of cottonwoods,
with the still shadows of firs,
wait,
for I am drifting down through
the clouded water of the Chehalis,
to be there with you,
standing
among stones, and mud, and sticks, and pierced leaves,
where we will see the pale silver side of a steelhead
passing by, upstream,
another winter gone,
and you
and me
so much closer to our father,
that river he has now become.

Stand there.
Wait for me.
I'm drifting, drifting down to greet you,
my brother.

On Christmas Eve in the Hospital,
My Mother Finds She Has an Enlarged Heart

We gathered, we came close
to reclaim kinship, that river
called Generosity
which sustains our family.
When she said
what the doctor had said,
in her eyes a bird flew over a field and
      dropped into the tall grass,
      terrified.

Because I now know
how we die daily of unexpressed affections,
I said:
      To us,
      it was nothing new; we'd always known
          she had a big heart.

Out of the sapped and withered grass then
the bird rose in her short flight.

There Is No Exile Where
the Heart Is Pure

for Pablo Casals

Behind the barn, the first week of March, on a bright
morning after long rain,
the windy cedar tree
turns round and round in the sunlight.
A winter horse
rubs himself on the corner of the barn.

Little pieces of cedar glide down where the ants are
calling home their old senators who
have failed utterly.
Coming home, carrying suitcases full of noise,
they pass through small American towns.

On the barn wall,
rusted nails bleed; and in fences, in hinges, in boards.
The horse (I think of Casals in exile!) plays
a suite unaccompanied in the silver cedar boards.
Inside the barn,
the stranded haywagon shudders.
Between its floorboards
seeds
trickle to the earth.

A dry dusty odor mingles with festering dampness,
and a hand—
        blue ridges and rivers coming and going through it—
rests on the white sheet of the windows.

My grandmother
comes to swing open wide the huge
double doors,
doors like drifting continents,
and a wedge of healing sunlight
slips into the barn before her.

Steelhead

The day I landed my first steelhead
from the Chehalis,
I saw a crow
zigzagging across Damitio's field
like no other crow has done before.

Answering, for My Brother

What do I do?
I show you barns in the air over Porter Creek.
Tulips that drop from trees in Venezuela
    and fall to the ground,
    bursting into roosters.
They whip the dust
out of small valleys under their wings.
Under the arches of their clawed feet
mountains blossom,
    distant but clear.

At the edge of ploughed fields
the surrounding sunflowers
march weary-hearted
heading into the cities of the sun.
Impossible not to follow them
and go with strange-shaped footsteps that
    might slowly turn bitter as green seeds.

Thin floating webs glide on the upper winds,
flash once or twice a dry silver fire,
then
    return to their invisible journey.

It is easy to see
    that among the insect world,
    many pilgrims have fallen to their knees.

Considering Poverty and Homelessness

Homage to Bashō

I cannot go back now,
    for what I have not done.
Of what is done,
take—and be kind.
    I am building a voice for my grief.
Alone, on foot,
if years from now I have learned anything,
    I will wander back.
Dust will rise up
on a dry winter road
where no one has walked before.

In Praise of My Ink Bottle

1

Life flows on, I go from place to place.
I carry this ink bottle with me
        wherever I go.

2

At the dinner table in some friends' house,
eating and drinking wine, I look down
and see the ink on my fingers.

Book 2

Stumbling Through Towns

Centuries Go By

In the world of men
centuries go by leaving
little trace.

A blossom in men is
like a cathedral,
seldom built.

It must be that in schools
when the blackboard is being erased,
under the sweeping hand,
     some words
     disappear forever.

Seattle in April,
Cloudy Day and High Wind

for Joseph Goldberg

1

Along Seventeenth Avenue, the trees
hold down big handfuls of old green
light, and the spring-time
is fresh.

From an upstairs window—

> over the alley
> over the tops of houses
> over the power poles holding up the weight of
> > so many tangled electric lines,
>
> and over,
> in the next distance,
> maples of the University,
> over a church on Fifteenth,
> above the trashy adventure of men in commerce,

the endless clouds
glide grey and white above the city,
immense
and changing,
ocean wind bringing them in
over the Sound, over mountains and valleys.

These clouds bring no rain.
They are carried on
as blades of grass are carried in ditches
> while no one sees.

2

In the miles and miles
of this city there is no house for me.
I remember peaceful moments,
away—

Thirsty, I go out to buy a sack of beer,
come back, park the car,
step over a fallen twig of cherry heavy with blossoms,
    it is time to go.

I sit in a friend's third-floor room, looking out.
There's the noise of traffic
and construction, huge
        concrete walls lowered into place.
A sickening blindness in everything.

I spend the afternoon
looking closely at the map: roads and rivers, and
mountains.

I wonder what it's like in the town of

    Wildwood,
    Washington.

"Storm Sinks Greek Ship, 281 Perish"

December 8, 1966
for George Hartwell

1

Oh no,
I said. It was the word "perish"
that cut my breath, and
the water laden with so many bodies.
Windows and doors opened and closed.
A storm of leaves fell.
Strong hands held the door.

I tried to think of them, then,
    in the stormy Aegean,
      enroute from Crete to Piraeus.
Two hundred and eighty-one
floating
face down
flayed with salt water
one by one growing heavy
dropping
down
into the dark field below the wave,
below the table with bread and fruit,
below even the great whale,
invisible in the blackness
who watches for a long time
a foot, a thigh, a torn face, falling and
disappearing into the greater dark below him.

I thought of
cold. Of water in the lungs,
    the peaceful feeling they say that comes
    with the first stillness
    when the blood goes slack

and the bones around the eyes fade away.
And for those still living
the body lies
fallen,
apple, branch, rag.

2

There was
"a crew of seventy-five commanded by
Captain E. Vernikos,
and two hundred and six passengers,
including one foreigner . . ."
"The foreigner was not immediately
identified."

The foreigner—
I might have stopped him on the street
as I did the postman today, to say
something absurd
about the weather, but
something that said there you are, and
here I am, it is winter, we
feel the snowy winds out of the mountains,
it is cold,
and we know that in the maple trees,
inside the buds at the tips of the black branches,
        there is long, long sleep.

3

When what is left of the foreigner—
        what fish and stranger creatures did not eat—
comes down at last

to the silent mud
where great treasures have lain,
    anchors of precious metal,
    chains,
    oar locks,
    stone jars that held
    grain, salted meat, and cool sweet water,
    companions of long journey,
down there
he nudges the mud in one place
to uncover the scarred metal, iron sword of Vikings,
touched for
the first time in thirteen hundred years.
Ending his fall,
he trips the leg bones of a fiddler,
    one of my ancestors, maybe,
    no sailor,
    who came along to see
    the white islands,
    the dark women walking with heavy jars on their heads,
the sun hot on his face,

the wind that crossed his ship,
his fiddle-bow that rode over the gut strings

    and made the song
    that brought him to lie songless
    in Mediterranean mud,
to perish . . .

East of the Mountains, Driving
to White Swan

June 29, 1969

1

The Yakima river valley
half an hour before the sun goes,
driving past farms
Sunnyside to Granger, and on, beyond Toppenish,
fieldrows of young beans, dark brown earth
sunlight on the sea of leaves over the darkening cornfields,
the hops growing up on high crossed sticks
    like ruins that disappeared
    leaving green arms
    clasped
    in the air.
I have a feeling anything will grow here; this earth
is rich
for everybody.
Small ditches filled with seeping water,
the land is peaceful.

On one farm, in fields of mint, between green rows,
white geese
are bent over like Chicanos
weeding the mint.
    Now and then one stands up,
    looks off into space,
looking at something over the tops of cars,
over houses,
far off,
    blue clouds over the Cascades.

This is the longest valley in the world.

2

At White Swan, out
　　beyond all the farms,
maybe a light every once in a while,
in the sage,
in dark ravines filled with willow brush,
under the newly risen
full moon,
　　the night is like deep water.

3

I'm getting here late.
This is
　　the first council fire in forty years—
　　All the tribes of the Yakimas are gathering tonight,
anyone welcome.

Following cars,
red tail lights in the dust,
a bright chilly night,
three miles out cars are gathered in a field,
white canvas teepees in a huge circle,
booths selling popcorn and soft drinks,
the bone game, and
a dirt-floor dance hall with
bleachers three rows deep,
everybody hunched up in the cold,

four Indian girls dancing off to one side, wearing bright
headbands and soft leather boots,
old men sitting around a drum,
　　eight of them,
calling for the next dance. The chief,

cowboy hat and braided hair, in the circle of
        seated drummers,
the face of a real Indian,
lifts the tilted bright silver microphone
        off his knees:
"It's a cold night, yes," he says.
"Dance and you won't feel it."

He starts to lift his drumstick, but
        picks up the microphone again:
"This is everybody's war dance!"
And the old drummers, dry and distant,
laugh a little and shift in their chairs.

4

Later, six men
from another tribe
with a drum come to play and chant.

These old men,
        are they
        the last?

Out there in the arena some wear feathers
        and dance,
        bending low,
        the sun rising on their backs
        circled by
        bright colored trembling feathers.

Here on the benches we all wear the same clothes
and have no bells on our feet.

Monday Morning in Everett, Washington

1

Taking a walk in the early morning,
in Everett. Not the most
beautiful place in the world.
Beyond the low buildings of the college,
black fir trees,
and beyond the trees, smoke pouring
from the high stack of Weyerhaeuser's mill.
In the old days of this town
sheriff, deputies, and townsmen stood on the dock,
their guns concealed, while the ship Verona
        drifted toward them,
            its engines cut.
The townsmen lifted their rifles then,
and fired.
A few Wobblies—
        working men who wanted to make a Union—
fell off the ship like shot crows
into the slack water, oil and sawdust,
chips of fir bark.

2

It is still going on.
This town needs
a saint.
Saint Everett of the Sawmills.

Out of the stack, dirty smoke
flows up into the grey, overcast sky.
Like a gaffed fish in an eddy,

a cloud of blood streaming out of a rip
    in the silver skin.

Here among the buildings,
sad architects are on the loose everywhere.
There are so few beautiful houses.
The town
is a stranded ship, a museum.
The houses along these streets now
are dying.
There are hardly any flowers.

Isaiah said:
    It shall be as when a standard-bearer fainteth.

If the angels of good heart are going to come,
let them come now,
burning the body clean, leaving
in our rinsed hands some flowers, the grass underfoot,
and the tiny cathedrals of song
where birds sit hidden in bushes,
    in the last living space
    between houses that are dying.

Americans Thinking of Religion

It is
they think
a 1937 Plymouth rusting on a creekbank.
Blackberry vines crawl through the windows.
Fieldmice
inhabit the back seat.
One tilted front wheel is sunk in the creek.
Rainbow trout
swim around the wheel,
    or rest
    in the dark shadow of the hood:
"God's true children"
heading upstream.

Grey Afternoon in Seattle During
the Viet Nam War

This is what it's like here.

The kittens look up from the floor like calendars.

Across the street, the Jewish family
is thrashing about,
I wonder what they're up to today,
making a movie maybe.
A couple weeks ago she asked me, that nice
neurotic mother—
please sir if you wouldn't park your car right there
my son he likes to park there
you know the poor boy just came from Viet Nam last week
they stole his tape deck and all kinds of
tapes, the poor boy you know he didn't get very much
money the army you know what they're like
and he just got back he saved his money
he didn't have a chance
to listen to them yet.

I said, yes, I'd move my car,
"No hard feelings," she said,
and I went away shaking my head inside
thinking
Jesus H. Christ.

Two Poems Against the Logging Companies

1

CROWN ZELLERBACH

"VIRGIN CEDAR"
This is not the tree ancient Aesop saw.
This is not the tree that was made into Spanish ships.
This is not the tall spirit the coastal Indian knew—
     Quinalt, Quileute, Makah—
     they waited out heavy rain
     under cedar and fir,
     waited,
     felt that peace,
     what was there.
This is not that tree. No.

This is the tree that the saw went racing through
head to foot, deafening the ears of sawyers.
This is where an endless string of quiet days went,
     "shot to hell."

Men in
business suits
from Boston walked through
these tall woods with gold
watches ticking in
     their pockets.

2

WEYERHAEUSER

Everyone knows
        about the rotten air of Everett, Washington.
Everyone knows
        how the fish go belly-up in the water.
But this town is a text Weyerhaeuser can't seem to read.
This is the book
that will close over their frail wings
and not open again.

Mean Dog on Country Road

Walking down from Harris's place on Grand Ridge,
singing aloud to trees on both sides of me,
I pass an ugly pink house
set in a little hollow below the road.
A police dog begins to bark, then
comes running through the junk-strewn yard,
and stops at the edge of the road.
As I pass along, whistling
and pretending that I'm not scared,
he leaps out into the road.
I will not look back.
The bark is close behind me when
a loud woman's voice roars from the house:
"Trouble, get down here! Trouble! You get down here!"
Bolting out of the eighteenth century,
Dr. Johnson flings open a second-story window
and leans forward, saying:

    "O excellently named creature!
     O most excellently named!"
One by one,
famous men step out from behind the trees,
to join me as I keep on walking,
each trying to outdo the other in brilliance.
I can't recall all the conversations,
but I believe you know them,
having perhaps been troubled yourself
on strange roads
that lead back to the city.

Spring in Ish River

I can hear the two robins
crying from an alder across the creek.
Above me,
in the vine maple, I see the nest.
I reach up and feel the four eggs lying lightly
among soft feathers.
I lift one egg out, lower my arm
slowly, and
stand still,
appalled: I see
the true shape of my hand.

Lament for the Ancient Holy Cities

to Deshung Rinpoche

In the lost valleys of a man's life
there is always
a small bird asleep,
sad creatures
alone at the edge of deep woods,
moving
like beads held in the hands of holy men,
       chanting endlessly.

A prayer waits.
A lonely warrior stands
       at the brink of morning.

Book 3

Love Poems

.

It Seemed Summer When Everything
Bloomed in Santa Barbara

for Susanna

It seemed summer, everything
sang in its turn and blossomed with a name.
We, on a high cliff over the Pacific
outside a small house, the ocean air
scented by jack pines in moonlight,
phosphorous waves over dark sand,
and in the still space between breakers,

      Newly come to love, I sought for words.

We leaned on the porch railing,
faced one another, then turned shyly away.
I remember the tall plant
blooming on the rising cliff, and
how we stood silent, until at last
you said its name: "They call it
the century plant, just once
every twenty years it blooms."

      Newly come to love, we needed signs.

"It's slow," I said,
"born as love is,"
heaven-bent emissary
bearing a homely gift of blossoms at its crown.
Beyond these praises, how do you honor
so long a labor: twenty silent years?

      Newly come to love, we needed words.

Far below us in the light-enfolded waves,
a waking gull stretched its wings
and cried.

I heard you say: "speak of the gift,"
and answered: "consider the burden
of twenty human years, and then rejoice."
        Newly come to love, everything spoke to us.

Still as the winds
moving through the pines,
moonlight shone on your face.
You drifted away,
and I was thinking of wild mustard and daisies
at home in the North, how they came
every summer to ravish the fields unfailingly.
        Newly come to love, we fall to memory.

I will praise this shyest blossom
born only in the mind.
"It would have kept Cézanne awake all night,"
you said, ". . . and Berthe Morisot
would lift her brush to touch canvas."
Just then, we turned
face to face, I kissed you
and saw a stranger blossom in your eyes.
        Newly come to love, we find ourselves.

In the Woods Above Issaquah

In the woods above Issaquah
near a grey farmhouse
we pick wild plums in the rain.
Another day, on Sauk Mountain,
we lie in a meadow. A bird
jolts a stalk of fireweed
so the light seeds drift over us
     and down the slope.
Far below, the Skagit River
winds toward the sea, turning
     like a pattern in old jade.
At home, you put some tomatoes
on the window sill to ripen,
and I think of jade again.
Nights,
while a bird outside the window
begins to budge the night away
     with a single sound,
your breasts, your lips, your eyelids
are delicate as petals of
     winter poppies.
I don't know what happened.
One night, no use knocking on your door.
I stepped down from the front porch
as rain fell through big leaves
and the grass woke up,
     and your face was
     a small round stone
     falling through dark water.

Sitting Alone at Night, Thinking
of Old Promises

Eleni

At night by the river
I see you fling your arms up into the sky,
    the moon visible between them.
There are no roots growing from your feet,
you float away.

The limb of a flowering tree comes down over a
    high brick wall,
the tip of a branch rests
    like the prow of a ship on water,
and sails on so slowly that in the morning when birds wake up
in the garden,
and sing,
an old sea captain standing on deck
far out at sea
    turns his head
    as though he heard them singing.

While drops of water
glisten on the mast and on the bright deck,
he lifts his dead wife up
once more
into the meadows of his heart,
as one day the flattened grass
slowly lifted the shape of her body
into the air.

He is like a young man again,
saying:
    "Summer has come by like a ship of blossoms,
    and if you call my name, I will

meet you—as I promised—
in the tall windows of the rose,
and hold you there, forever."

On This Side of the Mountains

On this side of the mountains, I found you,
and soon go back.
Tonight, shadows ripple over the coals,
and in me, your gift,
immense silence.
I hear a song I have placed my lips upon
for you alone.
I bring this old harp,
I unclothe it for you.

Over the mountains
ripening fields of wheat stand and wait,
and I have seen in you, suddenly,
your moon, your darkness,
and the sacrament they make together.
Because of your beautiful body,
and because you step
reluctantly into your nakedness,
I go like a white shadow
drifting through your darkness.

You are not alone,
and I have two hands.
I have made a home for you in my hands.
In one, a song.
In the other, someone far away
lies down and sees in mountain passes
a blue flower
lifting its green arms out of the snow.

"I will leave you to go there, but
not before I plant in your heart
the jewel of this night between us."

Pyrrha and Deucalion

They are given the prize of a child.
They have labored on the side of a far-off mountain.
Alone
Under pine trees,
She walks
On an autumn day,
The first of September,
The blueberries ripe.
When she thinks of Deucalion,
There are children close by
In the grass.
Farther up the mountain,
Out of stone,
Come blocks, for a home, or
    for a tower.

He sang frequently,
Low quiet songs.
Often a bird would be looking up at him,
He was so serene.
Watching the bird fly off down over the meadow,
Skimming the lavender blossoms of heather,
The fleabane, the fireweed, and the phlox,
He would see
Pyrrha
Coming up along the path.
Her walking made for him
An open window,
A song somewhere deep inside the house,
The scent of pine boughs on the table,
The wind in the night trees,
Her dress,
The sound of a small stream flowing
In the night between them.

Your Angels Go with Me Too

Your angels go with me too.
With so much of your gift mine,
why should I not return?
Whenever a feast is spread before you,
you touch the table. Your hands
turn the light inside them,
and hold it,
>   like moonstone,
>   like a flower.
Who was prepared for this—
Who was prepared for this!

The Widow

A mouse has climbed down
the wall, into
a coat
hanging on a nail,
into the sleeve.

The phrases
of love are long phrases.
Too long.

Two Seasons

1
FALL

What can I say to you?
A pheasant rises out of the grass,
       over the field
       into the dark trees,
              gone.

2
WINTER

In the abandoned orchard, winter apples
hang black in the moonlight.
Three deer
nosing the snow for windfalls
move under the trees
preserving with each movement
the stillness of
this windless night.

Spring Poem in the Skagit Valley

The birds are going the other way now,
passing houses as they go.

And geese fly
        back
   and forth
      across the valley,
      getting ready.

The sound of geese in the distance
   is wonderful:
      in our minds
      we rise up
      and move on.

3
The River with One Bank
Poems from Shi Shi

Dawn

1

In the early dawn
the sea sighs and turns over,
    wave waking wave
        all smooth skin.
    Whisper
    warm hand on thigh
       dip and rise of belly—
    the sigh of parting
    repeated,
    feast of morning dew
    riding the salt air.

In the beginning light I send out
words over the sea.
A word or two sets sail
out in the dark between waves.
Not even the night birds catch sight of them
    slipping into morning.

2

At full moon we were lucky,
not a cloud.
We saw the moon three nights.
After a day and a night of rain
the clouds still come now.
Don't see the sun at morning.
    Clouds, clouds
drop rain on the roof.
Door waits, window waits,

tree sleeps, flower shuts
and leaf-washed skin of morning
        brings day,
waking to the long grey raindance.

I can wait.
My feet are ancient.
And where my head was
is a seashell.

On the Way In

On the way out I'm silent
over the radiant path of mud and water,
     gravel and alder leaves newly fallen—
O summer,
        summer . . .
The rabbit nibbling some green leaf
keeps nibbling as I whistle by, sloshing,
     toes in mud—
(I love this mud, the deeper it is
     the better I like it).

I whistle my song, learned in the first
     days of June.
So now, going in and going out,
I whistle for the animals
so the bears and great slow
     movers of the night,
the birds too, will get used to my song.

Walking in at night
I'll whistle,
barefoot in mud, drunk
     and carrying a candle
     through the dark woods.

Now and then, ahead of me,
hear Shi Shi through the trees.

Out at Shi Shi

Out at Shi Shi
I whistled with the birds in the drift.
I drove them crazy, I think,
until at last I could sing like a bird.
I had my own song, like them.

There were days, searching
through warm driftwood,
barefoot and thriving on seeds—
When at first there were still
        some sad thoughts in my mind—
I stopped singing three days once,
while that great sea sang in belltones
        through my ears.

And one bird that loved singing best
followed me,
                teased me
        from a high grey log,
wakened me out of my sadness,
and I sang again.

Then I knew
        how they loved my song,
how they sang back, rich
                        and calling!

Tonight in the city, remembering this,
I throw my handful of burning coals
        into the air
and head back to the sea.

Salmon Moon

Surf
of moonwave,
        mist of dawn by the sea.
Mist of long lovely night ending.

The moon steps through the night.
It goes out into the south and west.
Wind comes out of the south and west.

Between sparse old shoreland spruce
        the moon is a silver wing
                in the clouds.

All night
the clouds drift over.
All night, salmon gather—
first of the run.

Fishermen in Neah Bay

1

Friday night,
Petroleum Creek on Shi Shi.
Late, ebbing tide,
moon a few days from full.
Chill wind from the north, clear skies, stars.
Fishing boats, mast lights stretched wide
    from the mouth of the strait—
        Juan de Fuca,
      fair inland sea of the Sound.

2

Talking with an old fisherman in Neah Bay,
cafe counter, orange coffee mugs.
Talk of ten-pound silvers,
    a few in the morning,
    five or six—
    lay up afternoon,
    head out at night.
Complaining,
It isn't what it used to be.

"Too many boats," stirring cream into his coffee.
"Oh, some alibi or other.
Years ago, you know, used to be only two outfits, it was
Larson's and Far West,
when I first came here to fish."
Waving his thick hand out the picture windows,
"None of this was here."
Boat harbor, breakwater, launching ramps,

bait, tackle, motor rental.
"All changed."

Smile, red face, baseball cap,
bright yellow flannel shirt, yellow slicker pants.
"Yah," pointing to his friend beside him,
a sad, silent man, Norskie or Swede,
shy, nodding,
"George can tell you."
"Yah," says George.
Then wants to get the waitress's eye,
"I kinda begin to wonder
what happened for the apple pie I asked for."

Rain Poem

Dark blue ship-of-cloud in rain.
Brief opening, flood of sun
  quickly gone.
Gusted surface of the
  grey-blue sea
breaks and flings spray,
  leaps forward: Mad women,
children, hands reaching,
  streaming hair.

Father of the Sea,
Mother of the Sea,
see how your children go.
   "Be loving, Be loving"
  cry of bird
   in wind and rain.

A Thousand Windows

I sit by the night fire.
And when I sit long in silence,
breaking time only with a cup of tea
now and then,
until at last it is time to sleep,
then I open and I dream,
and I wake again.
Fire crackling and settling.
And the sound of the sea is like
the feel of an open hand.

At night the sea is like a cardboard box
slapped down,
like a freight train,
a waterfall that suddenly dries up.
Mother quieting a child, father
drunk in his chair,
sleeping it off.
Like lovers in the beginning dawn,
bodies touch again. They wake up,
fall back into a dream.

The sea is like an elephant,
like a paper sack,
like a net of leaves flung into the air.
Like a man alone who
suddenly finds himself joyful.
The sea is like a glass of wine set down,
taste remembered—pool of grape
above the crystal stem.

The sea is like a thirsty widow,
a noisy hotel, a cold meal.

Letter slipped under the door.
Buffalo horns clashing.
Last page in the book.
Full starry sky after three weeks of rain.
The sea is like an iguana
running over a Persian carpet.
And the sea has a thousand windows
and not one of them is broken.

In America

In America, the sea brings up rubber gloves,
orange spots in the pure sand.
And egg cartons and grapefruit and glass jars.
Mahogany two-by-fours.
Cedar poles from Japan, strips of bark
     still clinging to them.
Immense old cedar logs logged long ago.
Peeled fir. Old shoes.
Boom logs with rusty chain.
Wire cable spools.
Legs of tables. Pillows. Whiskey bottles.
Boxes with names in fading black paint.
Why say it anyway?
Light bulbs.
Butt ends of logs stamped with the codes
of Crown Zellerbach, Weyerhaeuser
and Georgia Pacific.
Vinegar bottles with Russian labels.
Nylon rope, blue, gaudy green, yellow and orange.
And garbage from fishermen,
     grapefruit halves mostly,
     and instant coffee jars
overboard at night,
washed up
       into this pure morning.

Poem for the Naming of the Clearing
above Shi Shi "Never-Look-Back"

for John Utti

Climbing the trail up from
    Portage Head,
wet with morning rain,
    foot slipping . . .
How many have reached for
      this same branch!

Bear Poem

Saw bear tracks
this evening back from town.
A hundred feet from camp,
up under the salmonberry.
Wet spot,
wide, wide foot.

He turned off into the brush above camp—
    That's the noise I heard last night.
No berries now, hungry maybe.
So I'm down in the drift tonight,
on the dry sand, sleep here.

Fire falling,
put on some wood
and go to the creek, teapot in hand.
Driftwood giving off a faint light, the whole beach,
and moonlight on the running creek.

Dip the pot in,
water clean now after four days of sunshine.
Moon lighting boulders down in the creek water,
this last deep run of water to the sea,
silken and fresh in the moonlight.

Running into the Sea

I came here glad, needing no expectations,
and then, in full sunlight
the sea turned my body into glass.

At night, down near the waves, I stood
back to the bonfire, hot twenty feet away.
Saw my huge shadow cast up into the high fog
like a tree falling into space.
The waves leapt up out of the dark sea,
four waves breaking at once,
one behind the other
like a stairway being born in the sea.

Clothes off on a log.
Run through the orange light of the fire
into the surf,
water racing below my kneecaps.
Pushing against the sweeping water,
heading into it,
balls chilled through instantly.

Farther out yet, meet a bigger wave.
Turn and ride it in, white water.
Pick myself up off the shallow, sandy bottom,
outgoing sand between my fingers.
Up out of the shallower water, salmon jump.
Only ecstasy.

Flinging arms, hollering, voice
rising out of the ice.
Going out, greedy. Even this!
One more time and never the same.
Run up, feet thumping on sand, dodging

the black glistening stones,
into the fire glow.
Body alive. Body alive and naked water
all I need.

Friends

Friends make us fuller.
When friends leave, their light stays behind.
It is like the blue sea
that supports the white breakers
that come and go.

No matter how far I go,
I long to return and be with friends.
It is never the same fire I left,
but beneath it are the ashes
of all our meetings that have gone before.

Shi Shi

Shi Shi,
    promise her
never to leave;
come back
arms full of grief.

Shi Shi,
sound of silk curtains parting,
the rain-without-end
days and nights,
    one body.

All night,
the spruce-needle rain on the roof
Shi Shi
    Shi Shi . . .

Sunset

Spectacular, the word for it: sunset.
Pale sky like silk in the south,
and to the west,
thin blazing rays of sunset
like an enormous fan spread out,
      perfect as a shell.

Behind me, in the forest,
spruce trees stand silent and still,
like travelers
turning to look over their shoulders
struck speechless.
No day more radiant than this.

A solitary bat
comes out of the woods,
his small, blind, labored flight
etched above the afterglow.

Venus low in the sky
like a faraway campfire
      fanned in a light wind.

Autumn Equinox

Full moon sky.
When I die, peaceful, let it be
peaceful.
I hope I go like these waves
        breaking on Shi Shi,
wave rising out of the dark sea
turning suddenly white,
vanishing.
Wave after wave turning suddenly white.

May the song that comes of my dying
soothe the night birds;
may I wake myself, life after life,
in no less holy a place than this.

In the place between waves, especially,
Shi Shi, carry me
deeper into your silences.
Take me down
to the pure speech of whales,
down through swimming seals
        and schools of salmon.
Take me far.

When the first streams
        of swirled sand sweep over
        the white shell
        that is still falling
        through the dark sea,
take me with you.
Kneel down among the sea lice;
be there when I give my songs to the
        smooth round stones.

Be with me in the world of flying birds,
    the gulls
        and the ravens,
the songbirds among the driftwood.
Be with me on nights like this—
    I can hear the earth crying for a voice!—
Be with me when I sit looking out at the sea
    and don't know what to do,
some days helpless, some days
    like a lion rising.
While I go between these waves of
    day and night,
make the bottoms of my feet
    tough as hide, and
keep my back strong.

4
The Dancer

Why I Am Singing for the Dancer

for Alison and John

1

Inside the fat lady there is a beautiful
dancer. Any moment she will be
swept into the air like a feather.

2

She will turn and sail
slowly down, drift side to side, slowly
and with time to look around her and see
          no one watching.
Yet the joy she feels
began with the help of some
spirit that seems to be outside her
                              too!

3

There is a great joy in this.
There is the dancer,
and there is the one singing for the dancer.

4

And the song
comes in secret and takes
          the dancer's soul away.

The soul goes to a place
where a spirit with three eyes
        holds out a perfect body,
gives it to the soul that trembles,
fills up with color, spins,
        suspended in air, revealing
        a golden dancer at its center!

5

There are many, many dancers.
There are dancers
so powerful their bodies burst into flame.
They hold heaven in both hands
        while they glide round
        the great
        rock of the world.

6

There is the dance that lifts up the rug
        and shakes it in the wind
        and goes into the house satisfied.

7

There is a song that comes from
        high in the mountains
        and calls to the dancer alone.

The dancer goes up on the white mountain.

Tiny blue lights in the snow
        sing the song over
        again for the dancer.

How the Dancer Is Carried
into the Hall of Light

Writing With A New Pen, Seattle, Wa., January 22, 1979

1

I see this pen is
     full of ideas!
and this chair embraces
     heaven and earth.

The wide wide spaces
reach back
and the window celebrates,
bringing a feast of
light to the table.

This is the biggest gift!
The one I love most.
Makes ink flow out of
a pen, makes it say:
     "Everything that light
     touches
     you will speak of.

     You will
     bring up
     thoughts and scenes and
     memories,

     and you will
     lift them into
     poetry —

     the clearest light
     of all."

2

From the simple pen
that was only a while ago
lying on the table,

streaks of beamy light
shoot out now —
as though each thing shone upon
suddenly lighted up
        from inside itself.

Tell the scoffers
and those who linger in
doubts
whether light
        prevails.

"My pen is powerful.
My poetry is
clear and true."

3

As long as there is light
my pen will
move across the page

and the whisper of its
tip moving on paper
will turn into a great
lavish sound
        in someone's heart.

Looking into the face
of someone
       touched this way,
you will be
swept into the streams
of light breaking from
their eyes,

you will come to rest
on the lips of this lover,

and there be crowned
and carried into the
       hall of light,

break into dance,

things of the world
       behind you.

For this is the hall of light
and only the
dancer and the pure of heart
       find their way here.

This Flower

To Kenneth Rexroth
recalling his poetry reading
Labor Day, 1980, La Conner

Kenneth,
    you travelled all
      over reading
        your poems to
      us.

*

And now I am singing back
      to you!

*

His voice was soft
    for those in the back row.
    But it
      carried the sound of
        thunder through the mountains.

*

His love poems
    carried the fragrance of a
      fascinating juice.

*

Whatever the woman,
    a flower sprang up through the grass
    where they truly lay.

*

Ten thousand poets and ten
       thousand painters
             got together and painted
               this flower.

          *

It was a flower that
       obliterated
           thought from
             the human
                mind.

          *

It was a flower that said
       Get up! out of the
           corpse of your life
             —and dance!

          *

Neglect
    may
       come to
          this flower —
       but not for long.

          *

Every piece of paper that we
       used
           that came to nothing —
     Even that
      was
       something!

*

Kenneth, I saw you step
  into
    the circle —

    Now I want to be
    by your side forever.

*

No matter what
  there will be
    poetry!

*

ONE MORE FOR GOOD MEASURE

  Maybe exalted gestures will be
    retrieved in our time.
  Maybe our grandchildren will go through
    our trunks and boxes
      and be amazed.

HOME:

A Prayer for the World Where You Found It

for Tim McNulty

You fought for a wild river
flowing from the mountains.
When it reaches the ocean
rain is your blessing, rain
and a river that knows your heart.

"LIFT YOUR VOICE.
PICK IT UP LIKE A STONE, AND LIFT IT OVER
YOUR HEAD."

1.

Tim, you must have heard this.
You hold forth your voice, you lifted it
up to the rain and sun, to the clouds and sky.
And it is a stone inscripted with a prayer
for the world where you found it,
     forests and rivers
     fish and birds
          common to us all.
And farther back (up the Graywolf, say)
Animals that need people to give up
their mean and grasping intrusions,
the distantly murderous ways of men who
know nothing of nest or lair,
of how many creatures thrive in a mossy ravine,
or how the same bird flies in with a song
just when some berry ripens: —
Huckleberry shining in a shaft of revealing sun,
Mountain Beaver in the cutbank, where
an old logging road is healing over.
The places farther in where Bear
takes up her abode. Mother of Legends,

in a sleep beyond the world.
The Fox inside the cedar, roots feeling
the sky and dark wind a thousand years.
A long long range of hillsides where ancient mists
rise out of hemlock and fir,
vanishing in feathers of mist.
And toward the ocean in the West,
the sight is (all through the sky) Eternity
rolling like a gray stone in the waters of
great protecting gods,
Great Ones who divine in us
needs unmet among miracles; —
The sun by itself enough. And we get by
— all round the world! — with one Moon.
Plums! And houses! Hayfields, and
pear tree blossoms rising up in a crown
slowly drifting up to where a great hand
in the heavens greets the Gift returning.

2.

Down on Earth, in a small town,
off to the side, a little show on a wagon,
the big wheels painted
orange and red, holding up the traveling stage,
its purple curtains about to open,
the townspeople looking up: the flute and drum,
the clown and the laughing fool;
and they have a chance to see themselves, in
the wounded goddess and the healing angel,
and the wise man waiting to speak.

And out at the edge of town,
before the forest takes over, there are
fields at the prime of life, grasses rampant
and wild, wilder than the mind

when it has glowed so long at last
it can remember the first rain that ever fell,
and it knows where the first rays of light
fall on wet ferns.
And a voice whispers:
        Here's Home: —
Every green room of the forest planted:
Trillium and quince, alder and salmonberry,
and yellow Johnny-jump-up
with a leaf its own shade of green, and its stem
so thin it's almost not visible.
Spirits deep down in the earth giving themselves.
No place they turn their backs on.
And tiny white starflower taking up
so little room to say "yes."

3.

No wonder then.
The song of Nothing-Held-Back
goes winding up into the tall firs
reaching up between the tallest trees
to bind itself to the song of Spirit Birds
falling in thin streams
down from the sky-mountains of the world,
turning and turning
deep into spring, stirring winds in the lower branches: —
        Sky-flower,
        sky window,
        Cloud rain,
        leaf willow,
        moss water,
        fern wind (that one frond twirling
                        where there is no wind!)
Soul of delight, planted in home, blue and green.
And above it all

at nightfall
a strip of silver sky in the dark horizon clouds
shines through: —
One line of revelation put there
to be seen:
This is all we will ever have to love.
Here's home.

Here's Home!

November 1, 1988
Ish River

5
Joys of the Fluteplayer
Translations from the Swedish
of Rabbe Enckell
(1903—1974)

Spring

Spring is sitting in the shadow of a rock
beside a patch of snow.
With a stiff blade of quack-grass in his mouth
    he gives a whistle
so shrill
that the termite asks the ant
    "What's that?"
So shrill
that down in the slough
the mosquitoes start to dance!

Summary

At the window, the curtain
ripples—as if the wind were arriving,
hiding in its hands a present.
Magically, in broad daylight,
the spirit of summer awakens
in the silken weave
an absolute joy
that ripples through me like wind.

The Poet

The poet went into the landscape
and disappeared.
A pack of hounds, barking, followed
all the tracks
    and got nowhere.
No one found more than himself
and the others.
After a time, someone said
"Sad life."
And after a while, another:
"Meaningless poet."

Boxcar

I have switched in on the wrong track
and stand, a solitary car against the buffer.
How grey I look next to the edge of the golden woods.
I stand in the rain. Twilight deepens into dusk—
but for me, there is no departure.

Winter

Winter rummages around
like an old man fumbling in his pocket
among scraps of tobacco.

Joys of the Fluteplayer

for Aina, my wife.
You and I together, I want to call us
the fluteplayer's joy.

1.

That white room where desire sleeps
without dreams of blood.
The white room
where time has no murderous thoughts,
where no actual sun casts light,
you yourself are the light.
From there I'm able to see life
     dancing,
          beyond sadness.

2.

You lie in your black clothes,
your black hair streaming around you,
the faint softness of your features
     barely visible.
You are a child
     playfully hiding
inside her father's dark battlecoat.

3.

We took the city streetcar home.
Evening lay grey over the streets.
We rode on and your face was pale
as a lamp lighted before dark.
Your face was turned

toward the many stone houses
　　　along the street,
toward the people passing by.
My heart felt nothing for our destination,
　　only for you.
Then I saw your eyes come to rest
on a woman with a child in her arms.
O the great blessing of life!

4.

It is late into the night.
I go past many roads and houses
　　　looking for you.
I find you in your bed,
where the moon without waking you
glides across your face.

The sky is light like you,
the earth, beautiful like you.
Your hands rest in sleep
as though to receive salvation.

5.

I fall into you
like one who falls
　　into his own depths
to be purified.
I give my soul to yours
to be lifted up into you
like one who wants to be
　　lifted up into God.

Near you
all happiness is magnified
as through a child's eyes.
With you
everything turns to a play of sunlight
between clouds and water,
free of longing.

With you
my heart loses sight of itself
and seeks yours
so its boundary disappears—
a tiny insect
falling
from the tip of a tall blade of grass.

6.

My shining spirit
is made up of you and the spring.
My shining spirit
will walk through the year
    like an apparition.
It is free of me.
It is your creation,
bright redeemer of us both.

Matchsticks

*

My thoughts fly like quail
their widely separate ways.
My poem, my poem
I catch sight of you
a glimpse
before the forest and earth take you
in a sheltering embrace.

*

Driven by desire
the soul whispers
its most sincere love-talk—
as meaningless as
breakers between rocks,
more vague than water.

*

I'm not at home in this luxury.
The price tags on all your bolts of cloth
leave me cold.
What does it mean to be "for sale"
in that heap
where the fat bolts of cloth
    spread out
and the yardstick
barges forward, greedy
for elbow room!

*

A bird spins a lacy song
in the white sky.
It glistens brightly,
and a blue thread
hangs mute in the air.

*

These little matchstick poems of mine
make you smile.
Their harmlessness is the talk of the town.
But it's better to have a box of them
    in your pocket
than to sleep with ten fire engines
    in the living room.
And I'm satisfied
    if, when you strike them,
suddenly they light up my face
    and go out.

6

Bringing Friends Over
Versions of Issa, Buson, Bashō
and Friends

Issa

(1763-1827)

A new year—
 with new foolishness
  added to the old.

A few coins in his bowl
 and, as night comes on,
  the falling rain.

In my home village
 every flower I touch
  has thorns.

The first sign of a thaw,
 all of a sudden
  it's a village of children.

Beneath the blooming cherry trees,
 everybody knows
  everybody.

Mother swallow,
 the shack is yours—
  until the kids are grown.

A "booming economy"—
 there'd be room in my mush bowl
  for one more fly!

Don't ask me about people—
    these days it's hard to find
        an upstanding scarecrow.

Flower with nine bells—
    but here
        only four or five will bloom.

Another year,
    the autumn wind
        brings us closer to Buddha.

At night I remember
    the gate where
        I saw the violets blooming.

I was gone a long time,
    but in my village the cherry trees
        have kept on blooming.

All at once
    the snipe fly off,
        like that! years are gone.

Even the shadows of mountains
    shiver
        in the autumn wind.

Asked for directions,
   the farmer points
      with a radish.

Walking behind the plow,
   the crow acts as though
      he's the farmer.

Washing my hoe,
   so many ripples on the water
      startled the snipe.

The marshgrass
   rolls and turns,
      the spring wind goes its way.

A few violets
   all that is left
      to say who lived here.

Up here in the mountains
   even the moon
      shows up in the soup.

If it weren't for Buddha
   there wouldn't be
      this bright dew on the grass.

No business
    in this dirty world,
        the dew hurries away.

Don't cry, geese,
    in this floating world
        it's the same anywhere you go.

Buson

(1716-1783)

Petals of cherry blossom
    float through the rice seedlings,
        through the moon and stars.

The bright moon sails west across the sky,
    and the shadows of cherry blossoms
        go east, step by step.

It's a temple!
    this grove of trees
        and falling blossoms.

A line of calligraphy:
    wild geese above the foothills—
        and a red moon for the seal.

There they go—
    umbrella and raincoat walking
        and talking through the spring rain.

Deep inside the peony,
    the bee stays
        and doesn't want to go.

The peony
    drops to the ground
        two petals, three petals . . .

Along the caterpillar's back
　　you can see
　　　　the morning wind.

A wide ring around the moon—
　　is it the fragrance of plum blossoms,
　　　　is that where it goes?

A short night,
　　just a ripple of moonlight
　　　　left on the water.

A butterfly
　　came to rest on the temple bell,
　　　　sound asleep.

Mandarin ducks out on
　　the old pond—
　　　　the weasel just steals a look.

The bamboo broom—
　　fallen blossoms
　　　　swept away like dirt.

Spring has gone,
　　leaving the cherry blossoms
　　　　that took so long to bloom.

For the woman reading a letter
    by moonlight,
        light comes from pear blossoms too.

My wife dead,
    a sudden chill—
        stepping on her comb in our bedroom.

Together in the same carriage:
    me, and two whispering lovers,
        out of the rain.

Bashō

(1644–1694)

Spring again—
        nameless foothills
                in the misty dawn.

Now that the damn cat
        has stopped yowling,
                I can see the moonlight in my bedroom.

If you have no rice
        to give,
                put a flower in the jar.

In the cool of autumn
        some peel eggplant,
                some cucumber.

Ah! wild roses
        in bloom along the road
                for my horse to eat.

The best poetry is out in the country—
        farmers singing
                rice-planting songs.

and Friends

Silly scarecrow,
    right by your wooden legs
        birds are getting the beans!

                Yayū

The autumn wind—
    the first thing flattened
        is the scarecrow.

             Kyoroku

In the pile of branches
    ready for burning,
        leaves begin to sprout.

             Bonchō

The butterflies
    go back and forth
        stitching the rows of barley.

             Sora

A sudden rain,
    the newly opened leaves
        are singing with the tree frogs.

             Rogetsu

7

As Though the Word Blue
Had Been Dropped Into the Water

Seven Healing Poems

For Michael and Sandra Good

at Woodacre, on Paper Mill Creek
where I took the sun
and heard the healing waters
in Spring of 1984

As Though the Word Blue Had
Been Dropped Into the Water

The running stream
    is fragrant.

On the bank, in the shadows,
a small yellow flower
    with sunlight at its feet
puts my life together.

The little bird that is
    going to heal me
is hopping around in the bushes.

Set It Down, Carefully

I am the one that is being
        leaned on.
Something is expected.

Something that goes through me
        like something that goes
        through a tunnel
and
out
        into a field that contains
        the whole world.

My muse tells me:
        "Set it down, carefully
        in the young green grass."

Homage to Ryōkan

A little grey feather from somewhere
floated down onto my writing paper.
How frail!
    an inch long
    arched on its slim bone body
    more like a mist than anything else
    rolling over the white paper,
        soon gone
        a light wind claims it.
My only
visitor today.

Singer in the Shadows

Singer in the shadows, wake up.
A song is required that has never been before.
　　Come prepared!

A cleansing wind will announce you.
Afterwards, the sea will fall silent
and you will sing and then be lost again
　　as the sea commences.
A small stone set before the door of eternity
　　will recall
　　　　the day you were honored.

House of Many Ancestors

The face of the old luteplayer
    in the shadows.
The House of Many Ancestors
    where the lamps
    have been lit.
And people are becoming real once more,
    painting a picture called
      "The Feast That
      Includes Everybody."

A Dream Floods the Landscape

A dream floods the landscape.
Upriver, banks of earth
    crumble and fall
    into the flooding water.
An alder floats downstream,
    its roots washed clean.
Woven in the roots
there is a poem that says:

"Since you are going this way, too,
whenever and however it happens,
    bring your gift.
You will need to drink it like water.
Bring the flask with your name on it."

Like a Boat Drifting

Like a boat drifting,
sleep flows forward
      on the deep water of dreams.
Drifts and drifts . . .
until, finally
the bottom falls out of knowledge.

In the fragrant mist of dawn
the rower wakes,
      picks up the oars, sets them,
      and begins to row.
All night
he labored in his dream
      to be born
like a song in the mouth of God.

8
Shack Medicine
Poems from Disappearing Lake

Ink Bottle

1

Somewhere
    inside this ink bottle,
There is a starry sky!

2

Don't keep the lid on
    your ink bottle
Too long.

Early March in Town

for Barbara Cram

The daffodils are up
by the porch.
    One,
        two,
            three.
I could be next!

Laura's Birthday

One blooming
    skunk cabbage
upgrades
    the whole neighborhood!

Enough

Guiding a stray bee
    out of the house—
Enough work for one day!

Summer Solstice

for Allen Engle

It's been a busy day.
First,
    one hummingbird, then
Another!

The Frog I Saved From a Snake

The frog I saved from a snake
once, years ago—
Still here, he lives in a little
grotto, in under the Bald Island shore.
When I am out on the porch at night
washing dishes by candle light,
out in the dark I hear him.
Maybe he has wakened from a dream.
The first word comes slowly, but
it comes. Hello there!
Hello, friend. Boy wasn't that
some rain today!

When frog speaks, he knows I am
not a frog; that doesn't bother him,
                    doesn't bother me.
We talk anyway.
The love of rain is enough for us.

Shack Work

for Jeff Langlow

Shack work is good work.
After dark, around the table
we talk tools—

      good steel
      old wood handles

      what they do
      how you use them

      second hand
      or a gift from a friend—

Lightning in the mountains!

Thanks to Tony Morefield

What do you learn
on the river?
Free boots
always leak.

Ten by Twelve

for Erik Ambjor

My shack is ten by twelve.
    Two bottles of saké
    under the bed.

    Hot soup on the stove,
    and bread in the oven.

    My autoharp tuned up and ready.

When friends come rowing up,
How big this shack will get!

Lettuce Box

Lettuce box
on my floating dock.
Easy to tend, easy to water.

Thank you:
A head of elegant lettuce
        and a few red radishes.

And if there is no song,
I will search my heart again.

Eowyn

for Arthur & Ginny Greeno

Little swallow—
bundled up on an alder limb,
soft down still clinging to your wingfeathers,
feeling the wind for the first time,
    feeling the sun, too—
This morning from your nest
high in the old net shed ceiling
you looked down and saw the clouds
drifting slow on the water.
Now, you look up and see them
in the wide and endless sky.
And Mother and Father,
twisting their throaty songs into the air,
skim and turn and sweep, calling
to you: Try it!
          yes-yes-yes
            Try it! Try it!

Little swallow, river of life,
you make me glad, you
              make me glad:
Sitting on your very first limb,
Lifting your arms like a human child!

Herons and Swallows

for Rusty North

1

Long spells of heron-watching,
Now that the swallows have gone.

2

In April,
    when the swallows return,
The old heron will have less to do.

The Big Rain of August 1976

for Bill Slater

August rain
    windy as winter
keeps me inside the shack
all day tending the fire.

Out on the porch
I throw a sack of potatoes and carrots
    into the air.
My neighbor catches it, and
invites me over for soup!

Woodpile Down to Nothing

for George Durham, Boatmaker

Woodpile down to nothing,
I rowed across the river
and down into Beaver Creek.
Tied *Svalan* to a snag and
searched through the drift,
walking through cat-tails
    eight feet tall.
A touch of blue September flower,
marsh marigolds, and the golden
drift orchid speckled with rust
in the full mouth of the bloom
hanging serenely below the leaves.

Looked long for dry alder.
Not much new drift this year,
winter floods carried it off.
About to give up and search
some other spot, I found a
big alder: twenty inches through,
perfectly cured. Stove-ready alderwood!
Saw, chop, stack, and carry to the stove.
The river is good to bums and
    retired scholars!

I came back with a boat full,
big blocks of alder—
boat riding low in the water,
the wide river calm and inviting
in the high-tide evening westerly.

Rested the oars in midstream,
washed my sweaty face,

    rinsed my mouth.
Looked downriver, saw *Cloudwater*,
my neighbor's dory, in full sail,
    coming upriver to home.
Picked up the oars again.
Rowed homeward, too, singing:
    O glad for this dry alder,
    this living on the river.

Two Poems for the Good Given

for Jim Smith & Janet Saunders

1

My Father—
    He knew
How many beautiful August evenings
surround an ear of corn.

2

And my Mother—
    She knew that
Without love of Earth
there is no love of Heaven.

April has Turned Cold

April has turned cold.
The evening light fades through the clouds.
A string of geese calls me out
    to sing a farewell, and
I wish them luck as they go from Ish River,
away out over the ocean,
long long sweeps of rippling wings
    bound for Siberia.
Their wild song they take with them,
    and leave some behind.
They leave enough so
I don't have to leave home any more.

"Looking for Friends in History"

—Mencius

After a summer of shack work
I went to town and got my books.
Back home unpacking boxes
I quickly filled the new shelves.

Some old friends I recognized
right away. Others I go looking for
these cold mornings.
Where are you, Su Tung-P'o?
                    I want to know
what you were thinking
                    this time of day.

Frost in the marsh grass
and the tide rising.

Some Dust

for Jim Hartz

I bought a Chinese saké cup
    in San Francisco.
The man said it was
    a hundred years old.
It was not costly.
I liked it.
A small flower at the bottom
    with some dust settled there.

When I got home I found
the dust was not dust but
an imperfection in the glaze that would
    not come off.

We have to get over it in our minds!

Shack Medicine

for Dan'l Stokeley

The river glides in silence.
The night is deep, like a
    loving mother.
A silence goes back and forth
    through the marsh.

The same silence that was here
in my shack waiting for me.
    It was always here.

I was gone so long, now
the silence is so much deeper, and
    I sink down into it.

The sadness I met in the world
    falls away from me.
One by one my dreams return.

*

Everything good I put into my house
    is here,
        living in the silence.

Boards placed a certain way.
A window facing the moon.
A straight-back chair at the table.
Gifts received, and
    pottery bowls and cups
    I made with my own hands.
Things crude and useful that began
    from enthusiasm

and keep that life
and give it back.
Talismans and pieces of string.

*

In the night silence
my house speaks to me.

It leaves me alone
a long time, but
then it reaches out.

A gentle hand
penetrates my body.
Through the flesh
it reaches in, and on one rib
below my heart leaves hanging
a small silver box
with all my good dreams
inside it.

"Nothing can ever
be taken from you
now."

9
Ten Taos Poems

Taos Mountain

1

Early the light rises,
        sharp and clear,
        it stays clear as it goes along the warm
                        shoulders of the day.
Taos Mountain
keeps the morning light at
        its snowy round two
            highest crests.

Slowly through the day
        it gathers light:
        head, shoulders,
        breast, belly and thighs
        right down to its feet
        hidden in flared-out skirts
        trimmed with
        gatherings of
        native trees and plants.

2

The mountain
seems in its profile from here in town
like figures lying around a fire.

When you turn away
you can tell one of them
stood up and stretched and
        sat down again.

Her skirts, her blanket
made quick little winds
sweeping through the ponderosa.

Birds at Dawn

The birds have begun
      their morning song
rising lush and full
            from the dark.

From bushes and trees
they seem to be talking
to the night and
      the morning both,
balanced between them.

It is heartening to hear
      the birds.
Song added to
            song nearest it.

What else is here, nearby?
Blending certainty and song,
hidden in the light.

The Table I Keep

This is the table I keep.
This is my warm spot in the world.

A table to
rest my ink bottle on.
A table
with other tables inside it.
The ink wanting to be heard.

Ink whose body is a river,
whose fullness is
to be joined with other waters.

The ocean,
rolling landward
comes home
one river at a time,
cresting and breaking into song.

Each day at my table
I hear the heartsong
    and the lament,
as one by one
the rivers come home.

A Blanket

The cold weather is back.
It's moving in on a slow wind.

These days that have passed
    between me and the mountains,
these aged plateaus,
bearing the burden and
        wisdom of time,
make the blanket I'll wear here.
Blend of dreams and enchantments,
memories of home, too,
with greening meadows and
             singing swallows,
woven into what is here,
put by heart into the loom,
the blanket that
I'll wear over my shoulders,
and hold to me, like
a great good fortune.

Tears that fall on a blanket like this
are changed
just as
the day with its single star
becomes a night sky
wild with all the lights of heaven.

False Life

In the face of foolish enterprise,
the dwelling is never
                    big enough.
Greed and vanity are deposited in
          finer and
                    finer houses.

All your neighbors have money.
All your cars are made of
     robbed and desecrated
     nations.
Wounding the earth is
a habit you live with.

Living like this,
what you do
you do because you
     believe you have to do it,
not because it is
necessary to do.

A false life is deadening
to the doer and
the done to.

A stone falls on your head.
You stand with your mouth open
and nothing comes to help.

2

Maybe you will
believe something worth believing.

Maybe you will
wake up one morning
and find better shoes to
                         walk in.

Unless you find it within you
no path is worth walking.

Where things are right
there is a
path that is itself walking.
You will long for the path to go on.

     Even there
     you might find an abyss,
     and some old teacher
     pull you back.

All falling after that
will be what falling
you do in your mind.

The Ancient Peoples

Everyone has watched
     a spider
     making a new web, or
     repairing.

Everyone at dawn
sees the patterned strands of dew
between tall grasses, or limbs of pine,
        looping and
     heavy,
       held in the light.

I wonder about
     Anasazi, Hohokam, Mogollon
people of desert, plateau,
     and mountain.

Here from 2000 B.C.

Back when Spider Woman
     taught weaving

Back when potters appealed
     to Clay Mother
     and made offerings
     before the clay was dug
         from the earth

Back when baskets that took a year to make
had arms and legs
     and joined the ritual dances

When people sang for the ripe squash
        as they
        sang to children,
        and carried them home.

When the Wool Blankets Were Woven

1

When the wool blankets were woven

When the jars were painted, using
         blades of yucca plant

It could have been a plain blanket,
it could have been a jar with
    no figures on it,
or a grass basket unadorned.

Then where
would the lightning go to rest,
where would the streams
    remember to flow,
where would the willow hang its leaves,
what home would
     the mountain grouse have

How would the young woman
    remember her grandmother's hands

Where would wool go to be beautiful,
and a story go to stretch itself out.

2

The potter makes the world right, and
gives it one more thing to wonder at.
Brings in the dance, the pattern,
    the form and
    the elegant uses.

3

Maybe there were bowls and jars
that would hold too much
and were broken deliberately.

Maybe some were put away to be
        forgotten.
Maybe some were a binding that
        went wrong
and were carried away from the village
        and broken among rocks.

There must have been nights
        for some
        when the moon was too deep,
and the jar fell apart by itself,
        with no one near.

4

Otherwise, we know,
from evidence at hand,
satisfaction in work
        moved on through the land.
Every pueblo
            noteworthy for its pleasure
                        and skill, left its mark.

This Bird design made in one village
        and not in another.

This Havasupai basket covered with piñon pitch
made to carry water.

This small blanket
for the chief's granddaughter
                    at Tsankawi.

Rio Pueblo

Taos Mountain
    looks over the valley
and sends a river down
         water for the body
        music for the spirit
     at Red Willows.

I am far from home,
    far from Ish River. This year I
    see my first swallow
in the mountains of
    northern New Mexico,
flying
     above Rio Pueblo
in the afternoon sun.

Pueblo Songs

Your pueblo has a stream.
    You carry water
        for the blue corn.

Your mother and your father
wove blankets for
one another.

    You carry water
        for the blue corn.

       *

Your blanket
    and my blanket

and
the blanket
we make together.

No wonder the moon
comes over the mountain!

      *

What song was I singing
    that time I saw you?
I can't remember,
I can't remember.

It was cold and long ago.

      *

How fast the grouse run,
how high the eagle flies.

I am missing you,
I am missing you now.

*

Everywhere I go,
      I see you.
I was promised,
and kept you away,
I was promised,
and kept you away.

*

All night I have
followed the moon,
I have stayed by the fire, waiting,
thinking of you, silently
saying your name.

*

I saw you going to the water,
walking away
through the melon plants.

*

Among the blooming
melons,
the water pours
      out of a jar,

and you
sing

each time you pour.

        *

Your family visited again
when we planted squash together.
Every year we trade seeds.

Next year you will stay here with me.

To One Far Back in Time

A thousand years ago
someone prayed for the
rain that is falling today.

If I knew who it
        was, I would
turn now and call back
to tell them: *"it's raining."*

To that one far back
    in the darkness of time
I would say:
come, look
    in my garden—
I planted squash.
      Sturdy old blossoms,
enough light in them
to carry us both
      through the dark.

10
The Rest of the Way
New and Uncollected Poems

Five Oranges

for Mary Randlett

Nothing is lost.
One by one
the five big oranges
in a low bowl on the oak floor
disappeared,
a five-petaled flower
missing a petal each day . . .
This morning
one orange
rests deep in its center,
and the bowl
     turns to a blossom.

(1965)

Poem

for Paul Hansen

There are griefs I have not
shared with anyone.
This year, the leaves that fell
everywhere as they fell on my doorstep
had to fall without me.
It is winter.
And now I am in silent woods.
When I come out again,
past farms and many quick streams,
past scraggly tall alders
and the frozen web held in the forked limb,
before I do
I will leave behind me a small box
full of everything I feel about trees.
From your house,
we will walk back there together,
to the place of my last blessing.

(1966)

Mid-September at the Boomshack in Town

after a visit from friends

After so long,
        after a long time,
the well opens.
Friends pour
        their fresh water
            upon us.

Water of depths
for which no words
            exist yet—
only that
there does come this flowing
and this feeling.

When I am a long way
        down
            seeing-and-
            not-seeing
            all wound up together
in a tangle,
and can't make anything work—

one day
two strong brothers
come to my side.

Suddenly
the healing waters flow
            fresh and clear,
and just as suddenly
they are gone,
and I sit alone in the
        early sunset afterglow.

I'm inside a new body!
I'm jumping again
        full of love—

not for anything
but it lights up the
        man in the blue shirt
where he sits by the table,
pen in hand,
        all things embracing again!

At the end of my life,
I will lie down in
a little boat,
and float out on
the sea of
        these friendships.

Poem to the Parrot from Africa

1.

Sultry this afternoon in Seattle, hot
cloudless days, not used to it.
Downtown the businessmen's gills are beating.
Everywhere the businessmen's gills are beating—
They try to hide it in the bravado of
icecubes and gin.
But you walk back and forth on your limb
your feet clutching
like an old lady's hands.
You are beautiful.
Cool blue soft grey feathers
breast stippled
Your beak is a blue stone
drying in river sand.
Around your eyes, like a mask,
tiny white feathers flow together
perfect as lace.
Your eyes are
black iris
in yellow opal.
They do not look real.
Only the dusty blue eyelid (silk fringes
no hand will weave)
moves, giving away your life.
Be careful!
You are the Negro.
You are roast beef with
red tailfeathers.
You are the chicken no one will eat.
You breathe air dead with puritan goodness.
You were given, from parents traveling in Africa,

as a present.
They paid postage.
You endured the airplane, and the freight car,
     and the bus, and now
     the cars that go by on Newton Street.
Last week there were two of you.
Overnight at the vet's, too late. Your friend
     died, and went up in smoke over
Ballard.

2.

When I look at your feet again
I see they are roots covered with snakeskin.
And up through your throat, from your breast
     comes
a sound like dry crumpling paper.
     And then
you sneeze—
a soft baby-like sneeze. And I am
lost in your feathers.
I am the father who cannot
     reach for his children.

3.

Today you're in the house next door,
     in the hallway.
The house you came from is being fumigated.
Beside a vase of daisies and a poem of lost love,
     you say something, voice
        creaky
          like a car window.
Watch out!

There are men here who would make
        dice out of your eyes.
They would
peel your toes to make gloves.
And the people with aluminum ears will come
        to cluck you blind.
Some will even call you "Crazy Horse"
        and cheat you and lie to you
                then kill you
                        in secret.
You prince of the Sioux Nation!
You bright shoe lost on the stairway!
You are like a certificate that bleeds,
like a longing confessed too late in life.
And in Windermere, in "the Highlands" of Seattle
your face
is punched out in the shape of a monthly bill.
Once a month you arrive in the mail.
You are dollars; you remind them of
how generous they are, how
thoughtful.
You are sitting on a limb, in your cage
        in the hallway.
How can I
paint the colors of your cage?
What shall I say to
your mistress,
        who is kind?

Seven Thoughts under the Plum Tree

*visiting Paul Hansen at Al's Landing
just before the autumn equinox*

1.

You don't have to pull.
At a touch only
the ripe ones fall into your hand.

2.

The passing sun this September
      evening
casts shadows under the leaves.
Through the leaves the hand
glides to cup the falling fruit.

3.

In bright sunlit grass
      under the tree
a filled ring of fallen blue plums
lights up like
         a Monet painting.

4.

The ripest plums
      fall deepest
         into the grass.

5.

The bees and the yellow jackets
don't bother you
        under the plum tree.
In the last sunlight
they weave through the grass
        like harmless drunks.

6.

I may be drunk but
        those bees are
                drunker.

7.

Inside a really ripe plum
a yellow jacket
made a little cave to lie down in—
        dead drunk.

When I picked up the plum
he was sleeping it off
and just fell out
                into the grass.

Two Poems from Disappearing Lake

in homage to Gaston Bachelard

1.

Late in the full
            moon night
the wind
lies down &
            falls asleep
            in the marsh grass.

2.

Looking around my shack,
windows, shelves—
        gifts from friends.
Gifts that take a
long time to explain.

The house itself.

It will take a whole
        life
to explain this house!

Frog and Me, Election Eve, 1980

A small frog
    has come to live with me.
When I sing, he sings—
      and all in all
Frog seems quite satisfied
    with the way things are going.
Frog has a different look on the world.
Frog and me together
      here in the marsh,
we are easily satisfied.
    Simple food pleases us.

We go to bed when we want to,
we get up when we want to.
    And we feel that
      nothing essential passes us by.

      We are doing well.
So Frog and I will not vote tomorrow.
We don't know any of those people,
And they don't know us.

From now on I consult Frog.
In all matters of politics
I shall listen to friend Frog.

Frog is my president,
    my secretary of state
    and my supreme court.

Everything President Frog
    does is all right.
Frog is where he wants to be

and will hold no conferences
with anyone.

Frog says:
"There is not now nor has there
ever been, as far as I know,
any connection between the government
and flies."

Frog wants to stay home
and be left alone—
no taxes on his flies.
You see, Frog and Wisdom
joined hands long ago.
And nothing makes sense to Frog but
keeping a sharp eye out for his
bread and butter.
And turning a cold eye on
fat and stupid politicians.

Frog has been around, and is no fool.
Frog once sat on Thomas Jefferson's lap.
Sometimes on a rainy night
when Frog has had enough
he repeats what he remembers:
"He governs best
who governs least.
He governs best
who governs least."

Frog can talk religion, too, and
quotes from the Upanishads.
I am going to listen more
and more to friend and neighbor Frog.

Frog and me
will go places together.

For Friends Stepping into Marriage

Not looking back; remembering footprints.
Going forward, pushing branches aside.
The thought of treasure
    not-yet-conceived.

You find a rock by a stream.
Moss, and a poem that has
    just ended in sunlight.
Big hands have emptied themselves
        and gone.

Lie down in the cool wet ferns.
From now on
    you belong to the gods,
    "nothing to fear."

A drop of water
rolls deep into the fine hairs of moss.

God lowers Himself into the Earth.

The Rest of the Way

for Sally and Sam Green

Our fathers
carried us
a long way into the world.
They leave us one day, and die.
    And we carry them
    the rest of the way.

A simple path and wild roses greet us.
Dry grass sings the praises of water.
At dusk hills join together.
The woman-shadows and the tree-shadows
like the waves at sea
roll an old sad stone through the woods,
    grief wrung out of grief.

A cold morning and slowly growing light.
The birds start up,
one by one.

Three Garden Poems

Beetle

That beetle I saw
while I weeded in the lush and
    neglected flower bed—

I parted the growth to pull up
    the tall grasses, weed them out.

And there he was
moving over the cloddy ground,
every leg using everything it knew,
through tall stems of weeds and
under a high canopy of perennial flowers
    in bloom—

He had a portfolio tucked under
            his wings.

    *

By his walk,
it was plain he carried
all the secrets of his clan
with him.

A field of memories
    too big to leave behind
sent him out.
And here he has found
his field of plenty.

It's where
I do my gardening.

*

I'll say this:

I won't be the one to
shut this beetle out of
what was promised since
the rocks began to
        stand still
and the wind
brought its first soothing songs
                on the air.

If there is any rejoicing here
we will all do it
            together.

*

In the shadow of grasses
    of valerian
    geum
    foxglove
    and wild yellow buttercups,
    amid mint
    and sweet woodruff,

beetle goes along.

The afternoon light warms
    the path he has taken,
and I hear picnic talk—and
if I listen long enough
I can hear small accordions.

The stories they go home with!

        *

The longer beetle
       is here, the closer
our stories
become.

The weather stamps us with
its seal of approval.

"You are qualified to
linger a while longer."

"Sit down.
Write your letters."

Sun Shining through a Cabbage Leaf

I have maxims:

"One zucchini is enough
    for any garden."

*

"Plant for beauty first."

Nasturtiums climbing the corner
    alongside lemon cucumbers,
The bright purple veins of
                        red kale—
The vegetable peas with their
            white flowers
        showing where to look.

*

"Plant winter cabbage."

Next summer is when it
    reveals what it is really
    going to do.

It holds tiny pools of crystal water
on its leaves.
Afternoon light through the wide leaves
reveals the pattern of veins,
    a high and perfect geometry.

One form links with another,

the form
          varied but kept,
making a thing of wonder.

As the pattern repeats,
the form and wonder
          repeats.

The great palaces of the world
have got their message here:

The tiled floors,
the lace of stone windows,
the song confessing mystery.

All started here:

The leafy cabbage.
A dish singing in the light.

Lemon Cucumbers

Gardening, you know
when lemon cucumbers
    are ripe
by the usual signs—
a yellowish tinge
and the taste in the salad.

Also,
when they begin to
speak French. And Italian.

You hear them
    kissing summer goodbye,
beginning
their small poems
in its lingering warmth.

       *

At the tip of the latest growth
the vines hold
gold-yellow blossoms,

their own shapely
conclusions—
perfect odes,
bright testaments.

They say:
    We bloom not for
    ourselves alone.

Therefore
love enters the garden.

Afternoon Light

Afternoon light
    shining through
the flowers on the porch.
Through the open front door
    summer has stepped in.
My ink bottle falls in love
    with
    the world
        again.

"A Stalk of Grass Where the Wind
is Blowing"

On a stormy night in December 2001, more than 300 people gathered at the Arts Depot in Anacortes, Washington, to celebrate the life of Robert Sund. The crowd overflowed the main hall and filled two exhibit galleries as poets, musicians, Native American storytellers, artists and friends paid tribute to a remarkable life.

Robert Sund (1929 to 2001) was a poet, painter, translator, calligrapher, teacher and musician whose life and work touched the lives around him in profound ways. Like few I've known, Robert was a poet loved by his community. And his community was vast.

The crowd at his memorial was an unusual one for a literary gathering. Along with artists, writers and musicians were farmers, fishermen, carpenters, craftsmen and community activists, a broad, representative sweep of the rural Skagit Valley where Robert spent most of his life. All were touched by a poet whose voice and presence made the power of poetry come alive.

"It's surprising how many / people are laughing, once you get away / from universities / and stop reading newspapers," Robert wrote. The crowd that night paid tribute in fine style. Laughter and music shook the timbers of the old train depot even as the winter storm pummeled its walls.

Poetry for Robert was a way of living heart-first, and he shared his calling with everyone he came to know. He was an inspired reader of his poetry, and his presentations, which often included recitations and songs, attracted large, enthusiastic audiences.

Robert was a generous and gregarious spirit with a refined artistic sense that pervaded every aspect of his life. He surrounded himself with a few beautiful and functional things: pottery bowls and carved wooden boxes, Japanese tea cups, river stones and shells. He revered Buddhist teachings and was honored with a Tibetan Dharma name by Deshung Rinpoche of Seattle's Sakya Monastery. His paintings were in the "Northwest mystical" tradition of Guy Anderson and Morris Graves. His poems, calligraphed in India ink on art stock, were often given away to friends. He preferred to publish in small letterpress editions (a source of consternation to some of his literary friends). He considered readings more vital and important than publication. He could be prickly in the extreme. He could sing and play his autoharp until dawn.

In the three decades I knew him, visits to Robert were themselves poetic outings. Whether spending the winter with friends in town or living alone on the river, his residences were more hermitage than domicile. His small cabin at Shi Shi on Washington's wilderness coast was set back from the driftwood among windswept spruce, a teapot always steaming by the fireplace. His river shack, "Disappearing Lake," while only two miles from town seemed "far back" in time. A converted net shed on the Skagit estuary, it was raised on pilings to accommodate daily tides that flooded the freshwater marsh; access was by Robert's rowing dory *Svalan*. At his place in Anacortes during the last decade of his life, he transformed a small cottage in a friend's boat yard with an enclosed garden and courtyard of zen-like loveliness. No matter where he found himself, Robert lived an aesthetic life of beauty, simplicity and grace.

Friends joked that Robert was more suited to life in Sung Dynasty China than twentieth-century America. There's some truth to that. His poems reflect the influence of his revered elders: Sung poet and calligrapher Su Tung-p'o, Japanese poet-monk Ryōkan, the haiku masters Issa, Buson and Bashō. But as evident are modern influences: William Carlos Williams, with whom he corresponded, his friend Kenneth Rexroth, his teacher Theodore Roethke. As a poet who wrote eloquently of family, friendship and place, who engaged in community activism and became a spokesman for the bioregion he named the Ish River Country, Robert was American to the core.

Born (some might say prophetically) in the Depression year of 1929, Robert grew up in a Swedish-Finnish farming community in the Chehalis Valley of southwest Washington. Swedish was spoken at home, and as a boy he was immersed in a rich oral tradition of storytelling and song. His grandfather farmed with horses, "the best team of whites in Grays Harbor county," and Robert grew up within the traditional rounds and rhythms of what was essentially a nineteenth-century agrarian life.

This early experience shaped his aesthetic as a poet. He believed that poetry was first and foremost a spoken art form, and he could recite dozens of poems from memory. He also believed that poems should matter to one's immediate community. For Robert that meant the farmers and fishermen of rural northwest communities as much as his literary friends in the city.

In 1948 Robert entered the University of Washington in pre-med, supporting his studies by working summers in one of the last railroad logging camps on the Olympic Peninsula. An injury brought his logging career up short, and two experiences at the university derailed his future as a doctor. The first was organic chemistry ("I've had a lot of ridiculous ideas," he once told me, "and only failure has saved me"). The second was a meeting with his mentor, Theodore Roethke.

Roethke was a legendary teacher who received the Pulitzer Prize in poetry during Robert's undergraduate years, and his influence on Robert was profound. Both poets shared agricultural backgrounds (Roethke's father was a horticulturist) and early immigrant influences. The elder poet encouraged Robert to stay true to his roots and look to common, ordinary experiences for inspiration—lessons wonderfully realized in Robert's first book, "Bunch Grass." These gemlike poems of quiet attentiveness are dedicated to his teacher.

Roethke introduced Robert to the work of Williams, with its emphasis on spoken American idiom, and urged him and his fellow students, James Wright, Richard Hugo and Carolyn Kizer among them, to commit poems—theirs and others—to memory. Roethke also urged Robert to pursue his first language, and the young poet minored in Scandinavian languages, translating the work of Edith Sodergran and Rabbe Enckell among others. With Enckell, he found a kindred spirit.

Robert supported graduate studies with summer work fishing off the coast of southeast Alaska, working on a Native purse seiner the last year they pulled the seine net by hand. He described pulling nets in 30-foot seas, hanging on to the webbing as the boat climbed the swell, pulling like mad as it pitched into the trough.

These early work experiences grounded his poetry. They gave him an appreciative ear for colloquialism and and a compassion for working people that informs all of his writing. From farming with horses in southwest Washington, to railroad logging in the nearby mountains, to hand purse seining in Alaska and working the wheat harvest in eastern Washington, Robert was part of the original fabric of Northwest life in a way that few poets were. Gary Snyder comes to mind, of course, and Philip Whalen, both poets who knew and admired Robert's work. That Robert remained in the Northwest, living in small coastal towns, certainly limited his audience. But it gave his poetry a connectedness to place and community that nurtured him—and made him and his work beloved in the Northwest.

Among the poems shared at the poet's memorial, one from "Bunch Grass" seemed to capture both Robert's presence and the gift he passed on with his poems.

> *Near me,*
> *there's a flutter of birds passing through heaven.*
> *I'm singing in a silent place,*
> *remembering my happiest friends.*
> *I'm a stalk of grass*
> *where the wind is blowing.*
> *You have to*
> *bend close to hear*
> *anything at all.*

* * *

Tim McNulty
Lost Mountain
Spring, 2004

Made in the USA
Monee, IL
29 October 2023

45427533R00132